The Rainbow Bridge

By Pat Atkins

Copyright © 2021 by Pat Atkins.

All rights reserved. No part of this publication may be reproduced, distributed or transmitted in any form or by any means, including photocopying, recording, or other electronic or mechanical methods, without the prior written permission of the publisher, except in the case of brief quotations embodied in critical reviews and certain other noncommercial uses permitted by copyright law. For permission requests, write to the publisher, addressed "Attention: Permissions Coordinator," at the address below.

Pat Atkins C/- Intertype
Unit 45, 125 Highbury Road
BURWOOD VIC 3125
www.intertype.com.au

Ordering Information:
Quantity sales. Special discounts are available on quantity purchases by corporations, associations, and others. For details, contact the "Special Sales Department" at the address above.

The Rainbow Bridge/ Pat Atkins. —1st ed.
ISBN 978-0-6450876-9-7

This is the story of the many dogs in my life

Of the tears, trials, and triumphs…

Pat Atkins of Kismet Kennels, Western Australia

The Rainbow Bridge

Because of its many colours, the bridge connecting Heaven and Earth has come to be known as the Rainbow Bridge.

Just this side of the bridge, there is a land of meadows, hills and lush green valleys. When a Beloved pet dies, this wonderful place serves as their home. There is always an abundance of food and water and warm sunshine. Old and frail animals are young again, and those who have been maimed are made whole. They make new friends and play all day.

There is one thing missing from these carefree surroundings though, the companionship of their loving masters. Time passes and soon another day comes when one of them is distracted by a familiar scent. With nose twitching, ears at attention and eyes staring in delight, this one runs from the group…

You have been seen.

As you embrace, your face is kissed again and again and again, and once more you look into the eyes of your loyal companion.

You cross the Rainbow Bridge together, never again to be separated.

We Can Only Hope…

The Rainbow Bridge was the inspiration for this book.

Chapter 1

My very first memory of a dog entering my life was on a day that my Grandmother and I went to meet my Dad arriving home after he had been away in the country. He had been working on a big dam that was being built in Harvey in West Australia. As he stepped off the train at the station with his blanket roll over his shoulder I spied a tiny black nose followed by two black eyes emerging from the middle of the bed roll. I could hardly believe my eyes as I watched busting with excitement at the little puppy with black and tan markings struggling to escape his confinement. Dad had hidden him to escape the eyes of the train conductor as dogs were not allowed to travel in the carriages. A flash of instant love was there between Grandma, Nipper, and me. He was the first of several Nippers that entered our lives over my early years. One of these dogs created some problems for my poor Grandma. Children and dogs were allowed freedom to roam unsupervised in those safe far away days of the nineteen thirty's. Nipper was a fox terrier so as a breed they were hunters but sadly also killers of prey. The problem was that the only quarry around were the neighbours chickens. I was awakened one morning to the sound of very angry voices. I crept out to listen to the conversation, my Grandma on the defence saying "My dog would never touch a bird" this in spite of evidence of a mangled feathered corpse dangling from the indignant man's hand. Memory fails me on how the issue was resolved but I do not think my Grandmother was very popular in the neighbourhood, however Nipper survived.

Life was different for me after Grandma passed. She had been caring for me ever since I was three years old when my mother had disappeared from my life. When I was nine years of age I started to notice that she was acting in a very forgetful manner but I did not realise what was happening till two police officers arrived at my school to ask for details about her. Apparently she went to the hospital in a confused condition with no memory except my name and the name of my school to explain who she was. Grandma was put into hospital where sadly she passed away and I was on my own.

There was big change in my life after I went to live with my beloved Aunty Annie (My Dads sister) together with Uncle Tom Rafferty also cousins Joyce and Ronnie. They had been living on their wheat property in the outback country but came to live in the suburb of Cottesloe at the start of the Second World War in 1939. Several dogs came into my life from this time on. They brought with them much joy also quite a few tears. In fact I believe that I have cried more tears over dogs during this long life than over many other sad blows that life has handed me.

The first dog that came to live with us during my early teens was a cute little black long haired boy that we named Ming Chou as we thought he looked Chinese. He loved every one in the family but chose to sleep on my bed. He followed me around everywhere I went but sadly this led to his demise. Walking to the bus stop to say good bye to a friend who had visited on a quiet Sunday afternoon with hardly any traffic on the highway, I failed to notice Ming Chou following. He had wandered across the road to investigate something that had caught his attention. Much to my horror a car was racing around the corner hitting the little dog throwing him into the air screaming. I carried him home sharing his pain in my heart, till he died later that day. After so many years any photos taken of my early dogs have been lost but I still remember them very clearly. Losing my Ming was my first heart breaking experience but certainly not the last that I was to endure during my long life.

It was some time after the loss of Ming Chou that he was replaced in my life by another white terrier type dog. This boy was bigger than the previous Nipper variety with a much quieter nature. He was even a little bit lazy with his only tasks being resident foot warmer as well as companion house dog. We named him Beau believing him to be a handsome addition to the family. One morning I could hardly believe my ears when I heard people walking past chatting, laughing as they said "Look at that ugly dog". Ugly Dog, not my Beau, I took his head in my hands to gaze at him in wonder. All I could see was beauty, Oh! Well I guess the saying that beauty is in the eyes of the beholder must be true. I am not sure what happened to Beau as I left my Aunties care at eighteen years of age to venture into the wide world to see what life had in store for me. There were quite a few adventures over the years but nothing that involved dogs.

Chapter 2

My love of dogs stayed with me however, it was a long time before I owned my next one. This happy day happened after I had moved to Queensland from Western Australia. My family now consisted of one husband two sons plus one cat. This cat became very sick so I took her to a vet who worked at the Animal Care facility. Poor Puss could not be saved so she was put down. Wandering through the dog section I was thinking about the end of my cat's life and feeling very sad as I glanced into a cage to see a pretty golden dog that looked as sad as I was feeling, I had found my next dog Tammy. She was very thin so I built her up with lots of food until she became quite plump. She rewarded me by hiding under my bed to produce a litter of six fat puppies. I was in shock but everyone else was very excited. The pups were all miniatures of Tammy so I had no trouble finding homes for them. I took her to the vet's as soon as they were weaned to make sure there were no repeat surprises.

My Dad arrived from Western Australia for a holiday with my family in Queensland. He spent the rest of his life here, never returning to the West. This was a mixed blessing as I loved him dearly but did not approve of his life choices as he lived to drink. He was a happy good natured drunk but I hated to see him intoxicated and would get angry with him. One morning in August after I had spoken sharply about my disapproval over his drinking, he took himself off to the Queensland Royal Agricultural show, known as "The Ekka". On his arrival home that evening he wandered in with a six week old Border collie puppy in his arms. He had bought it for me from the prize winning litter at the show. He had heard me saying that one day I would like to have a pedigree dog, I had been thinking of perhaps a poodle or long haired dachshund."Itsh gotta pedigree ash long ash my arm" Dad informed me with a happy intoxicated grin all over his face, thinking he had made my dreams come true. What could I say? To me a border collie was a farm dog but I did not have a farm. How was I to know that this unexpected bundle of black and white fluff who was introducing himself by leaving a big puddle on my kitchen floor would be my ticket to a new exciting way of life? This was the beginning of a wonderful future of challenging adventures that would take me to the other side of the world all because of my foolish Dads love. I bless Him

Chapter 3

A few months later I was taking my three month old long legged Border collie pup walking on a Sunday morning when I discovered that the park on the beach front had been taken over by a Dog Show. The sign said "Waterloo Bay Kennel Club Show" This is very interesting I thought as it was an aspect of dog ownership that I knew nothing about. I stood gawking at people gathered together with many different breeds of dogs. Dogs were standing on tables while the owners sprayed them with water then brushed and combed their coats then checked the nails. It was fascinating to watch while the dog was picked up then placed carefully by arranging four feet evenly on the ground. The handler then dived into a pocket to produce an object to place between their lips. I watched in amazement to see a lady take something from her mouth and wave it in front of the dog while making clicking sounds. Apparently this was to catch the dog's attention to make him look alert. I later discovered that the brown object used was a piece of cooked liver (known on the show scene as bait). Little did I imagine that liver would become a very important item to me in the future? As I stood watching this entertaining spectacle a women came up to me to ask me about my puppy. I had noticed her grooming a cattle dog with her back to me. She had long jet black hair tied with a blue bow on top of her head. I had thought she was a plump young girl however at close quarters I could see that she was at least fifty years of age. I discovered later that she was a very well-known breeder of cattle dogs including Stumpy tails which are a rare variety of cattle dog. As we chatted she wanted to know who had bred my puppy, if he was registered, did I own him also was I was going to show him.

I could answer yes to the first three questions saying I don't know to the last one her name was Iris she became my mentor for the next stage of this dog life. Iris informed me, that I would have to join the Qld Canine Association to become an exhibitor, this she firmly encouraged me to do. She told me that she was the owner of the top winning Border collie named Patsy. I was very grateful for her helpful advice but little did I know at this time was that she had other intentions rather than being helpful to a stranger. Iris had exhibited Patsy at every show, she been the winning Border collie beating all others that came up against her. Gradually all her competition had given up, leaving Patsy with no one to show against. When Iris spotted King she was very keen to get him in the ring to give her an opponent to compete with as she knew she would be the winner with her superior contestant. We were to be "Lambs to the slaughter".

Following Irises advice I became a member of the "Queensland Canine Association," Now a certified owner of a registered Border collie dog that was entitled to be shown in competition at official Kennel Club shows. I was ready to dive head first into this new exciting world. Having received schedules of future events giving me details of costs as well as where and when each show would be held, the next step was to decide when it would happen. I had a phone conference to ask advice from my new friend to decide which show I should enter for my first dog day out. It was decided, the form all filled out together with a cheque for the entry money posted, then I had an anxious wait till the appointed day.

Our first Show, was to be held somewhere in country like surroundings and I had not been there before. My well-groomed King and my two boys were packed into the back of the car and off we went on our new adventure. It turned out to be a disaster as it was quite a long drive with King being sick all over the boys as well as popping off awful smells as we drove what seemed to be endless miles before reaching our destination. My two sons made an instant decision that dog shows were to be banned forever. They have kept to this ever since that day. I have often over the years heard mutterings of Mum and her bloody dogs from rest of my family I wonder why?

The rest of that show day is a big success with many sashes and ribbons to say that he was. My secret is that he was the only Border entered on the day Patsy was not entered at that show, in fact I never saw Iris show a dog that was not one of her own cattle dogs at any show from then on. Perhaps she had decided that our friendship was more important to her than winning blue ribbons. I hope this might be true. After the first show I became an avid exhibitor entering shows every weekend soaking up the atmosphere and trying my best to look like I knew what I was doing. I was the only one in my family to be bitten by the bug so I was on my own to get on with this project with minimal help from my husband Jeff. The next big decision to make was for me to buy a mate for King to enable me to breed some puppies and become a Border collie breeder.

King's first Show

Chapter 4

There was a man who lived near the Glasshouse Mountain's on a pineapple and orange orchard who I had heard had dozens of border collies. I sweet talked Jeff into driving me on the long trip to visit him to see his dogs. The decision to take this journey to meet this man was a very lucky choice as I found him to be a very special type of old time country gentleman that we both liked very much. Over the following years he became a good friend. His name was Horry Wilkes, every time I eat a slice of pineapple I think of him in that beautiful setting surrounded by his dogs with the mountains as a back drop. He passed away many years ago but he still lives on today in memory as one of my favourite people that were part of my life in the early days. I was able to buy a promising young female from him that I named Princess. What else? It had to be that or Queen as she was to be the mate for the King.

"Princess of Kismet Kennels"

Princess grew up to be a lovely specimen of the breed, well worthy of becoming a champion in the show ring. As months went by my weekends attending dog shows were also an education for me. I kept my ears open to become knowledgeable on all aspects of what was needed to win prizes in the show ring. I spent time researching attributes a dog must have to catch a judge's attention in order to be placed in front of other dogs in the line-up. Of course there was much more to learn about this sport that I would find out over the many years by observation as well as participation. Firstly the handler of his or her dog in the ring knows that it is very important to be able to get the best out of the dog. They must catch the eye of the judge, also to push the dog's good points and disguise any slight in perfections. Some smart handlers are very skilled at doing this I noticed as my education progressed. I learned that a standard of every breed has been set up for judges to study before they can gain a licence to judge any breed. This standard declares that to gain an award each dog must show as close as possible the perfect size, shape and movement of its individual breed. Then the finer points of how eyes and ears are placed, also the colour plus condition of the coat must be taken into consideration before the final judgement is made. It is not always easy to get all of this into perspective in order to pass the exams to gain a judges licence. Thirty years later I realised this when I decided to be a judge sitting for my first exam. I failed the first time I sat, but after a year of serious study and sitting again I passed the examination top of the class. I now had to take off my rose coloured glasses and read the standard for Border collies then look at my dogs with true judgement not blind love. King was too tall, did not have correct ear placement as they both flopped. He also had many other minor faults that could not be hidden. I came to the conclusion that he would never be a winner no matter how many times he was shown. Reluctantly I had to make the decision to stop wasting entry money by leaving him at home. Princess was my only entrant at weekend shows from then on. We both had fun enjoying the days outing as well the prizes and the compliments that we received from my many new friends. Princess was a popular winner; she was soon on her way to becoming the first Kismet Champion, as we did not have many border collies competing in those days.

Making the heart wrenching decision to find King a new home in the country to give him a better life with room to run in was extremely hard for me. I knew he was frustrated as we lived on a small allotment with nowhere for him to exercise except short walks to the park when I had the time to take him. I thought he would be happier if a special new owner came along to provide freedom for him to help him get rid of excess energy. I also felt mean leaving him alone when I took Princess to the shows. We were both lucky, shortly after I had decided to start searching for the right new home for King this ideal man arrived in a mud covered ute with country number plates. As we chatted he told me he was looking for a young dog to replace his beloved Border collie that had died recently. I introduced King to this very pleasant man, they bonded instantly. I was happy knowing that letting King go was the right thing to do. King hopped into the back of the Ute to go out of my life forever with not even a backward glance.

Chapter 5

Iris and I spent time together talking dog talk (as my family called it) we were making plans for the future. However fate took a hand. I had given up hope of ever producing a little sister for my boys after years of waiting and praying for the girl baby I longed for she never arrived. The day came that I decided that I was lucky to have three healthy sons I stopped feeling sorry for myself. I became grateful for all I had including my new exciting interests. I then discovered I was pregnant and my show days were curtailed for the duration of the pregnancy.

My next heart break arrived one early evening towards the end of my time when I sat down to rest for a few moments. Princess laid her head on my lap looking at me with pleading eyes. "Yes I know it's your tea time I will get it for you after I rest for a moment." I told her. She went outside to find the gate had been left open. I heard a terrible screech of brakes outside our house then a deathly silence. I knew my beautiful girl was gone forever even before I found her limp body beside the road.

I was devastated by this dreadful loss unable to believe that such a thing could happen. It felt as if my heart was breaking, I believed I would never recover from such a loss. Jeff decided after seeing me falling into a pit of depression to take me to visit Horry at his orchard to tell him my sad story. I could not stop crying on the long trip to the Glass House mountain's arriving there in a sorry state. Horry was very sympathetic kind and helpful; he gave me one of his special young females to take home to show. This generous gift helped me to resign myself to my loss. My new dog's name was "Pineridge Sally Anne." She wasn't Princess but she was there to help fill the big empty hole in my damaged heart. I believe that if the top breeders of border collies today were to look far enough back into their pedigree charts of present day dogs they would find this name. Sally had a very successful show career she also produced many top quality healthy litters.

Border collies are now one of the most popular breeds in the show ring. This sometimes worries me as these dogs are really working dogs with so much energy bred into them. When people fall for their eye catching looks, and buy them for pet homes, sadly sometimes they fail to understand this breed need so much more than most city dwellers can give them to keep them happy. They need to have a life that provides challenges for their active bodies as well as their brains or they often become a problem to their owners. It is a sad fact that many of these beautiful dogs end their lives in pounds or animal shelters instead of having useful lives in the country working. Now days I am very happy that many owners have turned to obedience training and other avenues of sporting events for dogs. These events are where the Border collie's natural talents as well as their energy and keen ability to obey orders have made them well to the forefront in many contests. Sometimes I wish I was young again so I could participate as it seems to be so much fun for owners as well as the dogs.

Chapter 6

After my baby was born I was laying in my hospital bed feeling very sad with a few tears escaping, when a dear little nun came to cheer me up. She asked me why I was so unhappy when the good Lord had sent me such a lovely healthy boy. I answered her with this information "I already had three other lovely healthy boys and I had hoped very much for a sister for them hence my disappointment". She had a few moments of reflection, then she replied that she believed six children would be a nice number for a family. I did not care for this idea very much so I told her that I would be going home to breed puppies as I could sell off the ones I did not want. I instantly realised I should not have shocked this sweet soul with such an awful statement. She took to her heels never to return. I expect that she went to the chapel to pray for my heathen soul.

As soon as I was feeling fit again I started to itch to try my luck in the show ring with Sally Anne. I then decided to start entering some weekend shows. It was a good for me and gave my spirits a lift. We enjoyed many winning days at shows my new girl proving her to be a worthy contestant, life was good again. Iris and I went to New South Wales to the Sydney Royal Show and came home with loads of prizes including the award for Best Puppy in Show. This was counted as a huge win so we were up in the air about that. I will write more about this trip later in his long epic. When the time came around to mate Sally I had to register a Prefix for my puppies with the Canine Control Council of Queensland. I chose Kismet for sentimental reasons. When we were young Jeff was in the navy, we spent a few days of his leave in Sydney. As we explored the city we decided to go to a theatre where a wonderful stage play named "Kismet" was being performed. We enjoyed the music so much we decided we would use that name for our first home. I submitted this when I applied for my prefix together with second and third choices as required and thankfully it was accepted. From that day on every dog that I bred would carry my Kismet prefix exclusively. This name I was told means Fate or Destiny. I truly believe it has been a favourable influence on my life bringing me good fortune and happiness.

When the time came around for me to explore my dream of becoming a dog breeder Sally was to be the ideal female to start off my future Kismet line of border collies. The season after she had gained her Championship title seemed to be a good time to put these plans into operation. The stud dog was selected and the deed was done. I was so excited waiting for the time to pass before the pups would arrive. Two months later with Sally due to have her babies my men folk planned a weekend away on a fishing trip. This left Sally and me to get on with producing this very precious package. I rang Iris to question her on what I should expect. She reassured me that all would be well but if I had any worries I could call on her night or day if I needed help. So I cleared the back room, covered the floor with piles of newspaper as instructed, to wait the start of labour. We waited all weekend, nothing happened. Sally relaxed and slept, I did not. She occasionally went outside to gaze down the driveway before coming back to doze again. I was a nervous wreck by Monday morning when the males of the family arrived home. Sally quietly welcomed them all in turn before returning to the whelping room to proceed to shred up all the paper to make a nest into which she popped eight perfectly marked Border collie puppies. What a relief! she had only been waiting till her human family had returned safely before starting in on the job of producing this very first litter for Kismet Kennels.

This picture reminds me of Sally Anne's first litter

I had a lot of fun learning the tricks of rearing my new babies and then how to part with them to their new owners. I had a few worries however I survived them and in time became a well-known breeder of top Border collie's and was producing healthy happy puppies that were to become good value to many farmers and property owners all throughout Queensland as well as many other places in Australia. They also sometimes were winners in the show ring when chosen for that purpose.

Chapter 7

Over the years I had many funny adventures and met so many different people because of the dogs. One that I remember did not bode well for a happy relationship with my husband Jeff. I had sold a Border female to a family that ran a sheep property in the country. They reported that she was a great help moving stock and they were very happy with her. They decided that it would be nice for her to have a litter if I would arrange a suitable stud dog .They made a special trip with her to the city for the job to be done. My top dog "Boots" was elected for mating for which he was ready and willing to get on with. The delighted family went off back to the farm to happily wait for the results. I believed that as they lived surrounded by many other farms that would need dogs to work the sheep so there would be a big demand for top quality Border collie pups. I was sadly mistaken. Farmers are often reluctant to pay money for a dog and wait till they are offered a free one.

When the puppies were six weeks old I had a phone call from the owner saying that she had no buyers lined up and pleading with me to help her sell them. I knew that I would have to get them to the kennels to do this so I worked out a plan to have Jeff drive me to the farm to pick them up. In my ignorance I had no idea of how far it was as she had told me it was the other side of Toowoomba. I had often driven myself to the Toowoomba Royal show which took me about two and a half hours each way so I told her I would ring from there for further directions. I coaxed Jeff on his day off to take me for a nice drive in the country, he rather reluctantly agreed and off we went

On arriving in Toowoomba I made the call for directions and it seemed that it would not be the quick easy drive to the farm that I had imagined. It was explained that it was a very long dusty drive on unsealed roads and it would take us some time to reach our destination. I could feel Jeff's anger with me starting to bubble up as he felt I had tricked him into giving up his nice quiet day off to go on mad mission. It was very quiet in the car from there on and after several hours of driving on bumpy dirt roads with several detours and missed signs it was very late before we found the farm.

Instead of the quaint country cottage I had imagined with lawns and flower gardens all around I found a shack with a tin roof surrounded by hard looking red dirt, there were not even any trees close by. Inside the house I was shocked to see hens and chickens wandering everywhere over the bare floors. The family welcomed us and insisted we stay the night with them as was very late. We had a meal with the family that consisted of the largest chop I had ever seen and a boiled potato. In the morning after not sleeping too well we set off for the drive home with six unhappy pups in a tea chest howling in the back of my van. Jeff was in a very sour mood and I am sorry to say this did not improve after a stone shattered the windscreen a few miles into the trip leaving us showered with glass and dust to drive many mile's to a service station to have it replaced. To top off this sorry event we discovered when we finally arrived home that I had overlooked the payment on the insurance policy so we had to pay full price on the replacement windscreen. It was a very expensive experience.

No, Jeff did not divorce me but it was close.

We had another adventure that resulted in a long unexpected drive but this time it had a much more pleasant ending. I had sold some Border collie pups over several years to an American couple who owned a huge cattle ranch outside of Darwin. I had met them when I was showing Borders at the Royal Show years before. We had met up several times over the years for them to let me know how happy they were with dogs I had sent them and they always said if we ever came to Darwin to let them know. My son Kerry with wife Gwen and baby son Jason had settled down in Darwin and in 1973 so we decided to have a holiday with them. I rang the American's while we were there and they came into town to have drinks and a chat with us, which we all enjoyed. I was happy to be asked if we would like to be taken to their property for a visit to see how the dogs that I had sent them as puppies had turned out. It was just down the track they told us and we decided that it would be a lovely extra addition to our holiday with the family. Down the track turned out to be several hours of driving in a jeep through drought ravaged country with very little to see and enjoy. However when we arrived I was delighted to see the homestead or as I was told it was (The Ranch House). It really was beautiful with wrap around verandas. There were green lawns with tropical flowering shrubs and trees for shade. We were welcomed with tall glasses of iced tea; this was something I had only read about in American novels. Our hosts seemed very pleased to have this visit with us and made me feel quite a celebrity and important to their lives.

After finishing our drinks our host took us on a tour of part of the enormous property. It was interesting but I felt quite depressed looking at mostly bare paddocks with kangaroo carcases everywhere. I was told that they had to be shot as grass for food was very scarce and they were in competition with the cattle so they had to go. The more cheery part of this inspection was seeing so many of my Kismet dogs working with the huge beasts that were being put into an enclosure; they were doing so with seemingly ease. I asked why they were using Border collies instead of the usual choice of cattle dogs for cattle as in the past I had only placed dogs on sheep stations and smaller farms. The answer that I was given was that he believed that my borders had much better temperaments and he liked them and had always been satisfied with the dogs I had sent him. So who was I to argue? This point seemed proven when the latest arrival was produced for evaluation. This was a cute little three month old male that obediently went straight to the enclosure and excitedly pocked his nose under the fence to show his interest in the great beasts in side. "Just look at him the proud new owner said fondly "He is showing off for his Mammy". Apparently he had passed his first test. This visit was a very special one for me as it made me feel happy that I was doing the right thing by bringing dogs into the world that filled a need, the bonus for me was to see it all happening with dogs happy heathy and doing work that they were born to do.

Sadly I do not have any photos from my visit to the Darwin American Ranch but this picture I found reminds me of what I saw the dogs doing on the day.

Chapter 8

The first trip to the Sydney Royal Show was a very exciting event for me but old hat for Iris as she had done it many times before. We were going overnight by train with four cattle dogs and one Border collie, all to be housed in dog boxes under the guards van. We left them for the night to settle ourselves in the train for the journey to Sydney. I was worried how Sally would fare, however they were all fine when we arrived at the station in Sydney. They were none the worse for rattling along overnight under the train. We were greeted by Irise's friends at the station as they were to be our hosts during the show. On the drive to the house, I started to think that they were a very strange couple as they seemed angry with each other making nasty remarks, this made me very uncomfortable. When we were alone Iris told me that they were always the same so it didn't bother her. She said they were obsessed with Shetland sheepdogs sparing no expense to have the best. Apparently they had plenty of money to do this.

When we arrived I had thought that even though the house looked like a mansion from the front but it lacked any luxury inside. There was only minimal furniture with mostly bare floors. I have since found this was quite typical for many people that were dog obsessed. Thankfully there was a bed each for us weary from travelling overnight, as well as sturdy kennels for the dogs. We were to go to the show grounds to show our dogs the next day so had time to get ready and have a look around. We were to be treated to some hair raising drives coming and going to the shows while we stayed with these people. One that really scared me very much was when we were coming home from the after show party with our host who was drunk and on the wrong side of the road most of the drive. However we lived to tell the tale arriving safely back home none the worse for the adventure. The bright side of this apart from all the prizes we collected was my very first sight of so many beautiful Shetland sheepdogs. They had been imported from all over the world but mostly from England. This is a lovely looking breed with a heavy double coat in various colours ranging from palest gold to dark mahogany with white on muzzle legs and feet as well as black and white and tri colour with tan markings and Blue merle. They are often described as miniature Collies but they are a completely different breed.

Two promising Kismet Puppies.

This is a short history of this *breed as it was explained to me.* The story is that an English dog enthusiast visiting Scotland in the eighteenth century admired these little beauties. He brought back a pair to be registered with the English kennel club. They were then added to the list to be exhibited becoming very popular in the show ring as well as house hold companions for wealthy dog lovers. At the time of our visit they were a rare breed in Australia. Our hosts owned so many and they were very possessive with them being terrified that another breeder would try to get their blood lines to beat them in the shows.

One little girl who was the latest import lived in the house. She liked my suit case, I often found her cuddled amongst my clothes when the lid was left open. I believe she wanted me to take her home. I wanted that as well but knew there was no hope for that to happen. I hopefully asked if I could buy one from them to be told that none were for sale. I think I must have passed some sort of a test because a few months after our Sydney trip I was very excited to receive a phone call to tell me to pick up my new dog from the airport the next day. I was to have a sheltie of my own. I was overjoyed to receive another beloved dog into my life. I would never have imagined that this day was to be the prelude of another heart breaking episode I would have to endure. "Ignorance is bliss" I have heard this saying many times and found it very true.

A Kismet Puppy ready to show

CHAPTER 9

A New Princess

She seemed perfect in every way to me, I was so thankful to have her in my life. She was up to show standard to win against any competition also to be my pride and joy at home for company. Of course there was a fly in the ointment, there had to be a reason that the owners had parted with such a potential show winner, it was that she was chronically shy and terrified of every one, this would rule her out as a show dog. If there was a chance to correct this fault it would take a great deal of loving kindness plenty of patience with long hours of hard work to gain her confidence. She would have to learn to trust me, to not be frightened of the world around her. This would be a tremendous task but the rewards would be worth it I believed. My stubborn streak came into play making me determined I could succeed at this task.

Meanwhile my border collies had become a band of six. We lived on a normal suburban block of land much too small for six dogs. It had become a problem to keep them exercised each day, to solve this we bought a covered trailer for the dogs to ride in. We would drive them to open ground where they could enjoy an hour's run each day. This became a chore so we decided to move to a property with a few acres of land. After a long search we found the perfect place for us. It was in rural Belmont on five acres of very pretty scenery with a small stream running through to a lake covered with waterlily's at the back of the property. There were hills and dales that made it all look interesting and many trees for shade. We all loved it. On this property was a typical old style Queensland house on high stumps with several sheds and covered area's that would serve as shelters for the dogs. I knew we had found the place to be happy, the boys were excited and there was room for the dogs to run. We found a buyer for the house in Wynnum and were all happy to move into our new home to enjoy a different way of life.

Getting back to my second Princess, she seemed to have settled down and was responding to my training which made me think she might be ready for the show ring. I took the chance and entered her in a small open show to try her out. All was going well, she was looking at ease until the judge walked up to her, then she panicked. This was big fail so there was more work to be done. About this time I had met a man who was one of the top sheepdog trial winners in the country. He was living in country New South Wales were we got to know him when we were visiting Jeff's parents to tell them we were expecting another baby. His name was Eric; he also bred border collies that he worked in the sheepdog trials. He told us that he would be competing at the trials with his dogs at the Brisbane Royal show in August. We invited him to stay at our home while he was there as we had plenty of room for both him and his dogs. I told him all about my problems with Princess and he informed me that he could train any dog even difficult shy ones of any breed. After Eric arrived I could see that he had his eye on my girl to help him prove this point. However she had other ideas. She completely ignored all attempts to coax her not even looking at him when she was with me. One fateful Sunday morning before the rest of the household stirred, Eric went to slip a leash on Princess to give her a lesson. Somehow she slipped her head out of it and took off down the drive way on to the road right under the wheels of a passing truck.

Disaster had stuck my life again. It was a repeat of what happened in the past. I was pregnant with my fourth son now my second beautiful Princess was dead. I could not imagine how I would be able to live through the pain of this another terrible loss. I have no memory of how I survived my misery. Somehow I found the strength to get on with my life but it was very hard for me. Even though sixty years have passed many tears are still falling as I write this. I have owned countless beautiful shelties over the years however none of them have replaced my two loves, a precious Border collie girl and Princess and my first beautiful Shetland sheepdog .They remain a fixture in my heart. Dog lovers believe that when a dog passes on, they go to a place where there is a beautiful rainbow bridge; there all our loved dogs are waiting for their owners. I do hope that this is true as I will have many waiting for me but leading the pack will be two Princess's one black and white and one with a golden coat.

Chapter 10

Many years slipped by before the next sheltie took up space in my heart. They were still almost unknown in Queensland so it was on a Sunday morning as I was scanning the dog section in the morning paper I noticed with amazement an advertisement in the Dogs for sale column. I could not believe my eyes when I read "Shetland Sheepdog Puppy's Four Males One Female for Sale." I was on the phone in less than a minute saying "The girl is mine sight unseen Please keep her for me". The owners were people who had recently moved from Sydney with two shelties. I was on their door stop within the hour to pick her up. It was wonderful to have a sheltie once again and I was thrilled with my new baby. She was a nicely marked shaded sable named Golden Treasure and she fitted well into her new life and was very loved by all at Kismet.

When she had grown into maturity and was ready to be mated I thought it would be a good idea to visit another sheltie family who had come to settle here in Queensland. I was hoping they might have an available stud dog so I took Goldy with me. It was a fairly long drive to where these people lived so before I knocked on the door I let Goldy out on the grass to relieve herself. Suddenly a flash of brown fur came around the corner of the house and Whacko! My girl had lost her virginity. I must admit I was rather shocked that the sire to be did not look to me the perfect sheltie but like it or not my first litter of Kismet Shelties were on the way. In due time the very special litter was to arrive and there were four more shelties in the world. I named the two I kept "Peter Pan and Tinkerbell". I had a lovely time with the only winning pair of shelties in Queensland for a year or so. As time went by other breeders started to arrive to show their dogs from Victoria and New South Wales against mine. At first I was not impressed by the new arrivals but I soon realised that it was my dogs that were not up to top standards. I had some serious rethinking to do and a new plan to hatch.

My border collies were doing quite well enjoying their new environment with so much more space as well as interesting places to explore. They also had many days to strut their stuff in the ring bringing home blue ribbons for me to hang on the wall. I had a favourite named "Boots" that I will write more about later as he played a big part in both Jeff's and my life for a while and not only in the show ring. We were to discover that this very loving and handsome dog had other more important talents to display to give us both some very exciting times for several years.

I knew I had to find some new Sheltie stock to restart my career as a top winning Shetland sheep dog breeder exhibitor at least in my own mind and small world. Knowing that there were to be Championship Sheltie shows following each other in sequence in Sydney, Melbourne and Perth, I decided on a plan of action. By flying to these shows I would be able to see what most of the top dogs were like. This would allow me to decide what was needed and available in order to work on a new line of show dogs in Queensland. By this time I felt I knew enough to recognise all the points of value needed to make a winning dog. Now all I had to do was to find and buy several new dogs that had all these virtues. This is going to be easy or so I thought and I felt quite proud of my reasoning. However I found that like the old saying "Pride comes before a fall" I was due for a fall.

Peter Pan was now a champion so decided to enter him in the sheltie section at the Perth Royal Agricultural show that would be held while I was on my Sheltie search. My Annie and Uncle Tom were very unhappy as their well-loved boxer Beau had died and was sadly missed. I would leave Peter with them to help fill the spot left by Beau. Peter had his last show appearance and much to my surprise was pulled out to win as best Australian bred dog in his class at this his final Royal show, going out in a blaze of glory. I presented a lovely sash as well as a Champion dog to my delighted Aunty and Uncle. They both adored this new addition to their lives caring for him so well that he lived to a remarkable old age of eighteen years. It was so rewarding to me that I was able to make my dear relatives so happy. I wept a few tears on my way home but I knew I had done the right thing by placing him in a home where I knew where he would be loved and cared for the rest of his life.

I have often been asked the question (How can you bear to part with your dog's when you are so fond of them)? My honest answer is that when they are living with me they have to share me with many other loved dogs. I want to reward them by finding a new home for them where they are the centre of attention not one of the mob. I would only part with them if I knew that they would be happy in a home where they would have the full love and attention of a family all to themselves or with only one or two others. I would never part with them to another breeder with lots of dogs. It has always been important to me to know I was doing the right thing by my actions both to my dogs as well as the new owners. I know perhaps this sounds a little bit peculiar especially to some other dog breeders but I lived with my conscience very happily.

*Good bye Aust Ch. Peter Pan
The First Queensland Champion*

Aust CH Trime Proud one

While visiting Sheltie shows all round Australia I had chatted with so many sheltie people who had dog's that I admired but sadly I could find no one who would help me in my quest to improve the dogs in Queensland. I was offered several that did not come up to expectations but none that would help me improve on what I already had. I then knew that I would have to change my ideas. I would have to take on a long term plan as the girls that I had were plain in appearance but sound in body. They both lacked glamour and the show quality that was needed to stand out in the show ring. So I made another decision which was to pick interstate stud dogs that had these qualities and use them to upgrade the puppies of the future. It would take a long time plus lots of money as paying out for costly flights and stud fees for my girls when they were ready for mating would prove expensive. This would also be very hard for me to put my trust in other people to care for my beloved girls and for them to send them back to me hopefully safe and pregnant. Not the quick fix I had been hoping for, however it all worked out over time. I did become a very successful Sheltie breeder with beautiful show dogs to be proud of also, to be recognised as the owner breeder of top "Kismet Shetland Sheepdogs of Distinction" It took a long time but it was worth it. I treasure the badge given to me that states I am a lifetime member of the "Shetland Sheepdog Club of Queensland." This was the club we started years before to promote the breed. I am so happy to know still thrives after so many years have gone by. One good thing that happened while I was in Perth that time was that I made a new friend named Betty and also I was to meet a magnificent shaded sable dog named Tryme Proud One.

"Proudy" as he was called was the image of what I had hoped to breed in the future. He had everything put together perfectly as well as a lovely temperament. He was handled by Cherrie (Betty's young daughter) who grew up to be a respected Championship judge as well as dear friend to me. I persuaded Betty to bring Proudy back to Queensland for a couple of shows and to visit with me. She had a son stationed in Brisbane in the Army that she would be able to see as an extra inducement to get over her fear of flying. It would be a first time for her and she was very nervous however with the help of a pill to relax her nerves she was in the plane clutching the arm rests with her eyes shut tight and we were up and away homewards. I was able to talk her into selling me a mature bitch with a lovely head that I hoped I could incorporate into my new line that I was planning for the future. So I felt that several good things had happened that made the expense of my search not a dead loss. Proudy was used at stud while he was in my kennels and he upgraded my future sheltie blood lines.

We had a lot of fun together and Betty enjoyed her time spent at dog shows and meeting other sheltie breeders as well as spending time with her soldier son.

When the time came for her to make her way home I was sorry to see her go and sadly we were never to meet again. Betty died many years ago from a brain cancer. Cherrie and I became close friends after I returned to the West for good and she now keeps her eye on me like a mother hen to make sure I am well and looking after myself in my old age.

Chapter 11

The boarding kennels turned out to be a success with most of the visiting dogs not creating too much trouble for us except that they annoyed the neighbours with noisy barking. The lovely quiet bush around our five acres had over the years become a fashionable destination to build huge luxury homes to live in. The people then commenced to complain that the dogs were barking. This became a problem for me as it was very annoying; there was not much I could do to quieten lonely dogs missing their families. My answer to the phone calls in the night was to say I was sorry about the noise but what did they want me to do about it. I could not understand why they built next door to a property with big signs out the front saying "Boarding Kennels" and not expect noise. I often stated that we had been here long before them. At four o'clock one morning I was awakened by a blaring horn with a women screaming out at the top of her voice "If I can't sleep you won't either"? I was very upset but what could I do? We decided to retire to my home state of Western Australia even though it felt like I was running away. All this happened many long years ago and the last time I visited Queensland I went to see what had happened to the property after I left and it was still there a going concern as a boarding kennel. I guess the people running it now were a lot tougher than me. Or perhaps all the neighbours had gone deaf.

Chapter 12

I had flown over to Perth to check if I would be able to have a life style that would make Jeff and me happy and found that it seemed to be a state that was ideal for dog people. Areas have been set aside especially for dog and cat breeders in several suburbs. This is something that seems to be unique to the West.

I found a suitable block of land in Canning Vale that allowed Dog kennels and bought it before flying back home to sell our property and move over. This proved to be more difficult than we had hoped. We found that there were many keen to buy such a property but unfortunately did not have the money to buy. The people who had the money did not want to do the hard work needed to run a profitable Boarding kennel. This problem took a long while to sort out but eventually we were able to sell to a lady who had shown dogs and was breaking up with her husband, or that was what we were told. We lowered the price and took off relieved to get going We bought a Toyota four wheel Ute with a cover for the dogs to travel in. Also a caravan with toilet and shower and set ourselves up with generator for running a TV. (These extras are at my insistence). Now with all these luxury's plus four Collie dogs four Shelties and one Bichon Frise we were ready for our trip across the middle of Australia. It was very enjoyable travelling the six days it took, staying each night well off road in the bush. The dog's would be free to have a good run before being given their meal and bedded down for the night. We cooked then enjoyed our meal after which we had a good night's sleep before starting off again next day heading westward.

When we arrived we stayed with my cousin Joyce and farmed our dogs out to other friends. Then we started on the task of clearing our block of land and preparing to build a kennel block and a cattery with a flat to live in while a two story house that was the last item on our planned agenda was being built. The idea of having a double story home had always been an ambition for both of us and we now had a chance to build one. This was not a good plan we discovered as time took a toll on aching legs climbing a flight of stairs as we aged. Of course all the building took a lot longer than we had hoped but eventually we were able to make it all happen. We were able to settle in and hopefully to be West Aussies for the rest of our lives.

After we transferred to Western Australia in 1983 and discovered there was only one other Sheltie breeder showing this lovely breed, I quickly decided that I would have to work on starting up a club just for shelties here in the West. This I did by breeding several litters of puppies to sell to people interested in having a beautiful dog. Each owner was recruited to be a member of the Shetland sheep dog club that I was planning to start; this was one of my more successful plans. Two years ago I was invited to be the guest of honour at the Sheltie National Show. This year it was being held in Western Australia. The event is held every three years with each state taking a turn with shelties coming to compete from all over Australia. It is a very exciting and busy time for the committee of the chosen club with every one trying to present a more spectacular event than the previous one. It was a very special day for me I was feeling proud that the committee had all worked together to present a really fabulous National Show. I was invited to be the honoured guest on the day and cut the cake in honour of the twelve year anniversary of the National Shetland Show. I reluctantly had given up working for the club and was no longer a member so it was very special to think that my part in starting up the club was still remembered by the present generation of sheltie people. It made me feel happy but a little emotional as my life had changed so much over the years.

I now had only memories of my previous hectic life that had been filled with exciting events and so many well-loved dogs. It was a wonderful day meeting up with people I had known over the years that I had spent in the world of dogs. I was also invited to the celebration dinner and this was indeed one of the most hilarious evenings I have ever enjoyed. For several years I had been developing a talent for painting. This was filling the empty space left after I had given up showing dogs. I was very pleased to have found a new hobby while getting to know many good friends in this my new life after my life of dogs. This enabled me to present portraits of Shelties that I had painted to be donated to the club to be auctioned on the night to raise funds. Wine had been flowing to create a free spending vibe and when the auction started bids kept coming till they reached amazing sums for all the paintings I had produced as well as all the other people's donations. This was very gratifying but I could not help thinking people who bought paintings might be sorry in the morning, but perhaps not as I have heard it said that most dog people are nuts. Perhaps this might be true as I have done some pretty strange things in the past at least in the opinions of my friends that are not dog lovers

One of my donated paintings

Cutting the Cake

Chapter 13

The Boots Story is all about my memories of a terrific dog that I could never forget. His name was "Lavettes Booties" he came into my life one Exhibition time (The Ekka) when many people arrive in Brisbane to show dogs at the Queensland Royal Show. One of my Border collie girls was in season, a stud dog was needed. I hoped there would be a suitable candidate amongst the dogs that were visiting that would suit my girl and that a mating could be arranged. I met up with a family from New South Wales that had brought several dogs to show and discovered that they were staying at a caravan park not far away from our place. With husband Jeff we went to visit to see what interstate border collies were like. We were both very impressed by a handsome young male that they called Boots. He had a lovely looking head with ears correctly placed, a nicely made body and solid legs. These were all features lacking in many of the Queensland border collies at that time. The owners told me that he was available for stud purposes but unfortunately the problem was that they would be heading back home before the girl would be ready for mating. I was very disappointed as I knew that this was the dog I wanted. However much to my surprise and thrilling joy the owner offered to sell me Boots. This was wonderful news to me. Naturally I jumped at this offer with Jeff in complete agreement. We both knew I had the best bargain I could ever have hoped for. Boots moved into my life and I never for one moment regretted that he did. He was to become a huge asset to me over time. We had our not so good moments but he was an easy dog to love and I loved him even though sometimes he made me very frustrated. "Boots" was a reluctant show dog. He was a very successful stud dog producing top quality puppies with every girl he was introduced to. The main one was Sally Anne; they were a lovely couple of dogs that I took pride in for many years. However I wanted Boots to do well in the show ring to be able to add Champion to the certificate when registering his progeny, but this would not be easy as I soon discovered. I had decided that this handsome fellow was good enough to beat any dogs that were being shown at this time. I was proudly prepared to have a quick run up to have a new Champion to add glory to Kismet kennels. Unfortunately pride comes before a fall and Boy! Did I again have a big fall?

I spent a great deal of time and effort to get him ready for his first show with big expectations on my part. He was moving like a dream, standing showing really well. I was so proud of him; I could not wait for the day to come to make all the other competitors jealous. The day came with Boots groomed to perfection. We went into the show ring to stand in line, in came the Judge. Suddenly Boots bolted out of the ring dragging me with him. "Shall I bring him back" I called hopefully "No keep going" said the Judge. I was very embarrassed but also very determined to succeed as I knew he would be worth the hard work needed to polish this rough diamond of a dog. Over time working hard with him, I managed to get him stay in the ring to be handled by the Judge but he did not like it one bit and he showed it. There was not the success I wanted for him, a sulky dog no matter how good his attributes, is not the one a Judge decides is the winner. I persevered but Boots did not catch the eye very often. One day Jeff made a rare visit to a dog show to watch the judging between Boots and a rival for the Challenge. Boots lost the contest. Jeff was outraged; then and there he decided to take a hand to fix this problem. He would go into the ring for the very first time in his life and show Boots. He did this at the next show, with a strong word to Boots Jeff took a firm grip lifting the dog's head firmly he proceeded to march him round the ring then stand him with his head held high. Much to my amazement he was awarded The Challenge. This turned the tide and success continued till Boots and Jeff gained the points to grant my sulky dog the sought after title "Australian Champion Lavettes Booties".

I made a promise to Boots that after he gained his final championship points he could retire from the ring as he hated it so much. A few years later I decided to take him on an outing to a Border collie fun day to show him off to the public. While I was in the ring showing a puppy I could hear a high pitch barking and I was sure it was my ring shy dog telling me he wanted to join in the fun. I gave his lead to a child to take him into the child handler's class where he performed as if he loved it all. It was hard to believe it was the same dog from past shows when I remembered the battles I had gone through with him. Good job I loved him or he would have been up for sale. Of course I was very proud of him although sometimes this was tested. We had started up a club to check if the border collies being shown these days still had the instinct to work sheep. To do this, we gathered all the dogs from our newly formed Border collie club to introduce them to some sheep at a property owned by an interested sheepdog trial man. Boots came along and was tied up while the other dogs were tried out. After all of them had a turn with many different degrees of satisfaction I proudly took in my "Champion Lavettes Booties," to my utter shame Boots was terrified when a quiet sheep came over to check him out. He cringed down in the corner trying to get away. Everyone but me laughed their silly heads off. With a very red face I tied him to the fence while I went to get the young pups to see what their reaction would be. After some time I noticed a look come in to Boots eyes watching the sheep as he slowly raised into a working crouch at the ready. I then happily realised that a future sheepdog had arrived. One day as the men were practising for a trial at our place where a trial ring had been set up in the side yard of the property. A dozen wild rangy sheep had been purchased from the sale yard to test the trial dogs. There seemed a lot of swearing going then I heard one of the men shout to me. "All right Pat send out your bloody Boots". I let him off from under the house where he had been confined so he was not able to interfere with the training. Off he went straight down to where a stubborn whether had bailed up refusing to go through the gate. Boots went up to it and nose to nose pushed it backwards into the pen. This is what the prize winning trial champions had been trying and failing to do but it was no trouble for Boots he was a strong natural sheepdog with a good eye.

Pat with Boots

I had found out quite a lot of information about how different types of dogs worked when used to control sheep while chatting with farmers when they came to buy a new working dog, I was getting to know much more about the life that any dogs I sold to the country people would have. This gave me more confidence in the fact that my stock was being bred for important reasons

TRAINING on their five-acre property at Belmont, Pat Atkins puts Boots through a short practice run. "If you go on too long a dog becomes confused," she says. The short stick she carries is only for signalling, and is permitted in sheepdog trials at the Show.

THE AUSTRALIAN WOMEN'S WEEKLY — August 4, 1965

One day before the 1965 Brisbane Exhibition I was contacted by "The Women's Weekly" magazine asking my help to make up a story with photos of me training for the sheep dog trials that were to held be held at the Exhibition. I tried to tell them it would not work as I was not competing but was talked into it.

Boots and I were ready on the selected day with me waving a stick and trying to look as if I knew what I was doing, Boots was keen to go. The camera man and reporter arrived, and we were on our way to become stars of the "Women's Weekly magazine August 1965." They took lots of pictures of Boots working the sheep with me strutting around looking important . My little son Leon with a litter of puppies got into the act as well. The camera man and reporter thanked us before leaving me to wait for the magazine to come on sale. The magazine came out at last and we were to see that it all looked good. This gave the kennels some terrific publicity for the boarding kennels that we were planning on building as soon as I could raise the finance to start this new venture.

LEON ATKINS, 3, clutches Debbie, his favorite in a litter of ten produced recently by Mrs. Atkins's border collie Sally Ann. Sally Ann has had 41 pups in four litters and lost only one.

Leon got into the act as well as he loved playing with the puppies. This was helpful to develop good temperaments. He was never happy to see visitors looking at them as he was frightened that they would steal one of his playmates. I have saved these pictures that were taken and published in "Women's Weekly" August 1965.

One day after a huge storm a red pigeon fell to the ground wet and exhausted close to where Boots was sitting. I was amazed to see the dog pull the bird between his front paws and start to lick it dry It was such a strange thing happen that it brought tears to my eyes to see a dog being so gentle with a bird. From that day on Boots and the pigeon became close companions till the sad day that Boots died. I never set eyes on the bird again after that day. As the years went by my dear old Boots was going deaf as he slowed up with age. His habit was to go over the road from the property to do his business every morning. One terrible day he did not hear the garbage truck that hit and killed him.

The sad thing about loving and owning a dog is that their life span is so short compared with ours and he was lost before his allotted time. I was very upset to lose such a beloved long-time companion and grieved for him feeling that it was such an awful shame that my magical dog's life had come to such a horrible end after being such a star all his life. Looking back on my time with Boots as well as the many other special dogs that passed through my life I feel very grate full for the fact that they all were with me as I enjoyed, cried, and survived the many experiences in my life of dogs.

__Goodbye Boots my special mate__
__Till we meet again at__
__The Rainbow Bridge__

CHAPTER 14

The next dog that is part of this story did not really belong to me as she was a gift to Jeff from Eric, while he was staying with us while the Royal Agricultural Show (The Ekka) was on. He was competing in the sheepdog trials and Eric had entered a smooth coated female named Rosy. Jeff drove them to the show grounds to watch the trials for the first time. Rosy and Eric completed their round in record breaking time winning the competition. While they were driving home Rosy crouched under Eric's feet to push out a tiny black white and tan spotted female puppy. He named her Ekka and gave her to Jeff hoping that she would follow in Rosie's footsteps. She did eventually but only after Eric took over her training after suggesting that Boots would be the best one for Jeff to learn with if he wanted to follow the trials. Jeff decided that he did. Together we set up a trial ring on the property and bought some sheep from the sale yards for Jeff to be educated on how to trial dogs. We invited other trial men to visit to use the place to train their dogs. They often gathered there and it made for interesting times as well as educational for Jeff. He never really got to be very good at this calling perhaps because Boot's understood what to do. The dog would quickly get the sheep into the pen ignoring Jeff's orders so loosing points along the way. Poor Jeff was never to win a trial but we had some very happy times following the Sheepdog trials all-round the outback of Queensland and New South Wales. We followed the circuit during the season which was the lead up to the big one at the Brisbane Royal.

Ekka was a lovely dog, perhaps not the most beautiful in looks compared with my show stock but quiet gentle and faithful, she had a litter to Boots that produced three smooth and three long coated pups. One of these pups became a top trail winner for Eric; Ekka then lived out the rest of her life as a companion for Jeff. When it was time to enter the dogs section of the Exhibition I put some plans into operation. I decided to start up a campaign on the virtues of smooth coated border collies as working dogs for the country. I advertised in the show catalogue as well as on the benches where dogs of both types were on display for the general public. When I was not running round the ring performing for the Judge's attention, I was talking about the dogs to every interested person who stopped to admire them. It was a busy tiring day. Sadly for me my time effort and money was wasted as the Judge put every smooth coat I showed to the end of the line. It was not very successful either when the farmers came to me for a replacement for their retiring working dogs. They would not have a smooth coat and would only settle for one of the "Bloody Good Kismet Dogs" that they always had when they wanted a replacement for an older working dog. I suggested that the smooth short coat would be better especially in the harsh burr country. The answer I got for this argument was that coats were no trouble as the dogs got sheared when they did the sheep. Well OK! I know, it was not one of my better ideas but I lived and learned from my many mistakes. I once read that we come into this life to learn many lessons. When we come back to a new life if we have learned from past experiences we will be one step up the ladder to perfection. Perhaps this is true so I guess I will keep trying to do the right thing but I will take more advice before jumping into what seems to be a winner in case I fall on my face again as I have done many times in the past

Our friend Eric died from cancer at a relative early age. I believe it had developed because of his employment that was for the most part baiting dingoes (Wild Dogs) in the country. This was a service needed as the farmers were losing live stock from their properties. He was paid for this service when he produced evidence of the scalps to be counted. Years later it has been discovered that the poison used was a very bad one that causes cancer. Can you imagine the irony? A man whose whole life was the love of dog's and the outback should die a sad death because he had destroyed so many of them.

Eric's two daughters Patricia and Jennie were in my life for some time. I believe I was a stand in mother to be a sounding board for the many drama's that growing up throws at young people. There were many of these and I suffered along with both girls through many upheavals in their lives before they both moved away to get on with their lives. Many years have gone by since those days and after losing touch for all that time I was thrilled to receive an e mail from Jennie some time ago to say she had been thinking about me and was grateful for all I had done for her when I was in her life. I took this to be the answer to my prayers, when I had pleaded to God for a girl. He gave me the chance to experience what it could be like to be a mother to two girls for a few short years. I have been blessed by this for a short while . I have been given a different path to follow with my dogs. Perhaps I have not have been designed to be a fulltime mother to girls. I must confess that I was far from a perfect mother to my four boys as I am sure they would tell me if I asked. I only have the knowledge that my dogs and perhaps sometimes my husbands and a few good friends loved me. I give thanks for these blessings.

CHAPTER 15

My Magnificent Colies

This next episode I believe was the most enjoyable in my life of dogs. It all started when I was showing a sheltie at the Sydney Royal. While standing waiting for my dog to be called in to be judged, I noticed a male tri coloured collie being paraded for the judge in the adjoining ring. He caught my eye standing but when his owner started to run him round the ring he moved with such a smooth action, it as if he was flying. Falling for him in a big way I could hardly wait to meet the owner of this lovely dog. Her name was Mary I was told that she had imported him from New Zealand and that she would be mating him when she returned to Queensland at the end of this show. A new plan began developing. When my husband asked me what he could buy for me for my birthday, my immediate answer was "One of Mary Rand's collie pups". "Good God, haven't you got enough dogs" was his reaction. Of course I hadn't. The happy day arrived for me to pick up my very special girl puppy she was to be named "Brongia Boronia". She was a perfectly marked golden sable, growing into as far as I was concerned, a perfect specimen of the breed and a delight to live with. I was in heaven again. The day soon came when Bonny (as I called her) was three months old and she was entered in the first show as Baby Puppy. It was a big surprised to find that Mary had entered a baby puppy as well to compete with mine. On the day I had come to pick my puppy, this twin had been hidden as Mary had decided that her choice was the best one of the two even though she had promised me "Pick of the Litter". I thought that this was a little sneaky on her part but I had the last laugh as this judge picked Bonny first with Mary's in second place. My Bonny went on growing into an even more beautiful show dog with the sweetest nature. I loved her for that as well as that she was perfectly at ease enjoying the outings moving around the ring with the smooth movement of her magnificent sire that I had admired so much in Sydney.

Brongia Boronia became my first dog worthy to become a Collie Rough Champion making me so very proud of her. When the time came for her to be mated I had decided to use a very handsome golden sable male who was very much admired as a top show winner. The owner of this boy lived in the country so it was more convenient for everyone that he pick up Bonny on his way home from the show for the mating, bringing her home the next weekend. This would enable several mating's during the week to ensure a good outcome. Feeling worried and nervous about trusting any one to care for my precious girl I had to let her go off to meet the future mate. When she was brought back home the next weekend I became very angry with the tale I was told. It was that the fancy male that I had decided to be the groom for this "Royal

Wedding" did not fancy my beautiful Bonny and he refused to get together with her. This was hard for me to believe. The owner had decided to introduce her to a young tricolour boy for the mating. He thought to do this so I would not be disappointed. Boy! Was I mad, I was really upset? I was sure that as Bonny had a tri colour sire, then to be mated to a tricolour there would be a litter of black pups. This I certainly did not want.

Two months later Bonny produced a beautiful bundle of eight golden sable pups and one tri girl. I sent out a silent apology to the stud dog and the man responsible for the mating for having such cranky thoughts about them. Three months later while I was fighting with the sable girl I had kept from Bonnie's litter trying to get her to walk on a lead, with not much success. I looked down to see the little tricolour girl watching the struggle. It then went through my mind that I should try to train her in case someone wanted to buy her. As I slipped the lead over her head and I was expecting her to go into fighting stallion mode on her back legs as her sister had, to my astonishment she looked up at me then walked quietly beside me as if I had been working with her for weeks. My next thought was tricolour or not this girl was made for the show ring with no effort on my part. She was a keeper. I named her Magic Moment (Maggie) she was a joy to me in every way. I was so happy to have her become my special girl who would be my most successful entrant in my show career as well of being a loving companion for me till she retired to live in the country. She was only one of many special Collies that I was so happy to know I had brought into the world to bring pleasure to many lives my own included.

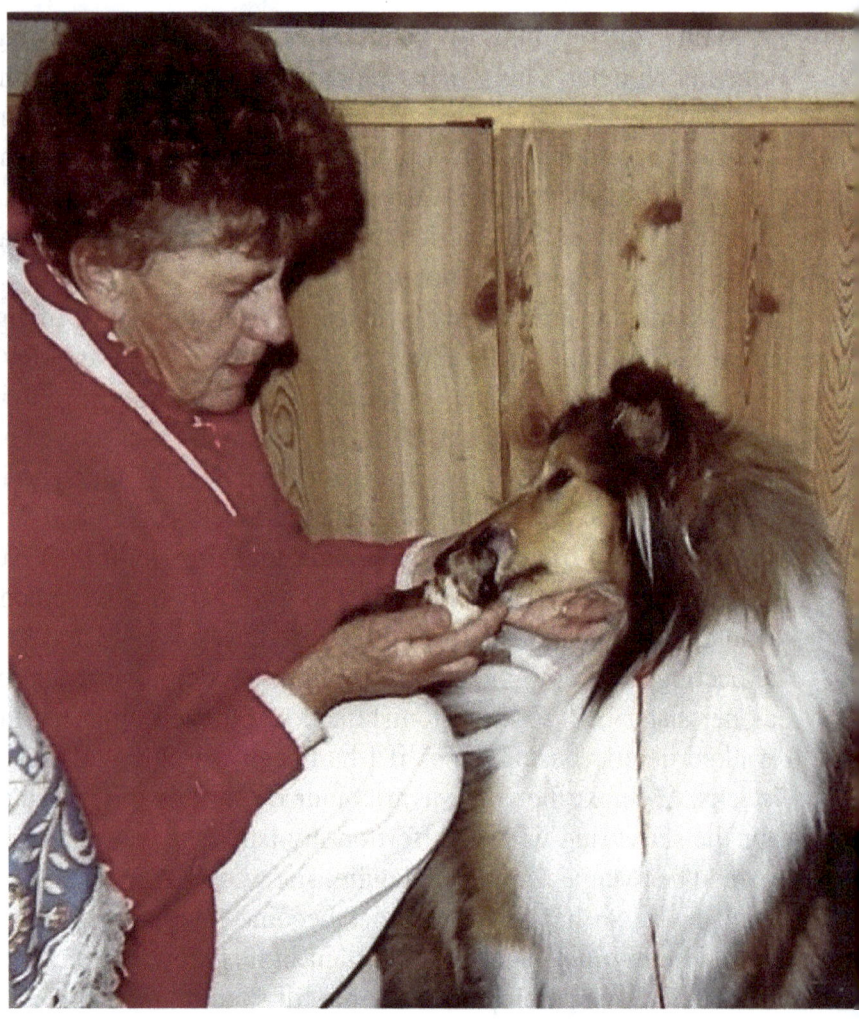

An early morning Surprise

Chapter 16

Jeff retired from his work as an operator at the Ampol refinery. He had been suffering for several years with heart problems and had a huge bypass operation nearly losing his battle to live. I knew if he continued to work in the stressful condition of the refinery I would not have a husband for any length of time.

I started to plan on relocating. I decided that it might be a good plan to go over to my home state of West Australia, I hoped it would be a good move and Jeff agreed. I would be near my beloved Aunty and Uncle as they were getting frail in their old age. I then flew over to investigate and was happy with what I found.

It was very gratifying to find a nice property in a designated dog breeding suburb, something that is unique to the West. I bought it, and then flew back to Queensland to sell up and start a new adventure. It took a very long time for us to find a buyer for Kismet Boarding Kennels. I discovered there were many people who would love to have a kennel property but most of them did not have the money, the people that had the money did not fancy the hard work it took to run kennels. However eventually a person who had show dogs and husband trouble (Or so I was told) offered to buy us out. By this time I was keen to sell even though I had to lower the price.

We prepared for the trip to the other side of Australia by buying a new Toyota four wheel drive, a comfortable caravan with a shower as well as a toilet at my insistence. We even had a TV run by a small generator. The dogs all settled down in the covered back of the Ute and we were off across the Nullarbor with four collie's four shelties and one bichon Frise. We really enjoyed the six day trip, staying well off road each evening giving the dog's a good run to exercise them before bedding them down at night. We then cooked and enjoyed a meal before having a good night's sleep, and we were ready in the morning to set out early for the next day of travelling westward

After arriving in Perth we stayed with my cousin Joyce, the dogs were farmed out to friends we then set out to build a house, kennels and a cattery. This took many frustrating months but eventually we moved into the first part the completed, cattery which had a flat attached. Then the kennels were built and at last the two story house that both Jeff and I had always wanted, now we were able to build one. We then settled down happily to become West Aussies for the rest of our lives

This was the new "Kismet W.A". I had brought some lovely dogs with us that far out classed the local dogs being shown at this time. It was so convenient that the show grounds were very close to the kennel area where we lived, after the long drives I had to take to get to show dogs in Queensland. I had a lot of fun bringing out my beauties at each show but I tried to take the wins modestly as I really wanted to make friends not jealous rivals. It took a bit of diplomacy but I soon discovered that some local judges preferred looks that they were used to so I didn't always win. Before leaving Queensland I had two pups that I had decided to keep I had named them Maggie and Cohan. These were to be the two that I had chosen to take back to Queensland to enter in the Royal Show at Exhibition time after we were settled. The boy was a present that I was giving to my son Scotty. The two collie Pups and I flew back to Brisbane to stay with Scotty who was very happy with his new dog but not too excited that I had entered him into the show the next day. I gave my old friends a big surprise by arriving back, coming all the way from Perth.

My puppy was the first in his class to enter the ring and I found I was standing beside my old rival Mary. She had recently imported a dog at great expense from England that she hoped to have success with and here, he was my competition. My boy was quite unperturbed by his first time to him, very strange surroundings. However he acted as if he had been there many times before. He caught the judge's eye and was awarded first place in class and puppy in the group I almost felt daggers in my back from Mary as her pup had been placed second to him. I must have a big mean streak as I was not a bit sorry for her, even knowing that she had paid thousands of dollars to be trumped by an unknown pup from Perth. She tackled me later saying that my dog had upset hers in the ring, that was a big lie. Answering her I said (with tongue in cheek) "I am so sorry Mary he does not know any better as he is only a pet." If Mary ever reads this I hope she forgives me and knows that I am eternally grateful for the joy that she gave by selling me my first beloved Bonny to be the beginning of my never to be forgotten family of Collies. Maggie also did well in the show ring I was so proud of both of them. I took Maggie to the Adelaide National Collie show later that year, bringing home trophies and a silver cup inscribed as Best Puppy in the 4th National Collie Show. I think that was the best highlight of my dog life with one of my own dogs

After all this excitement I settled down to enjoy my improved lifestyle. My dogs were able to bark all they liked without me getting complaints from my neighbours. That had been a big problem for me in Queensland as I hated the thought that I was annoying people. Our home on the quiet secluded five acres where we had been living for many years had become a sought after area for wealthy people to build their huge luxury homes. Several people had built close to us then complained about noise from the kennels. I was woken many times by people complaining and once at 4am by a loud car blaring outside my bedroom window. This was followed by a women screaming at me that if she could not sleep I wouldn't either. I was very upset and I asked her how could I keep lonely home sick dogs quiet and why did she build next-door to a boarding kennels when there were large signs declaring "Kismet Boarding Kennels". Now I was here in the

West surrounded by other kennels I did not have that worry. My weekends at dog shows were now only a few moments' drive to get there instead of travelling hours to country shows. Life was not the hectic one it had been instead I felt more relaxed, relieved, and so pleased that we had made the decision to change states. Jeff and I both thought we would enjoy living here for many years into the future.

My best dog at this time was a golden sable that I called Beau. He was a lovely looking boy with the habit of holding his tail high when I took him around the show ring to show how happy he was to be there. Nothing I said or did would break this habit. In the end I gave him to other people to show and he was much calmer with them.

Beau flying his flag of love at the Brisbane Royal Show

Maggie winning BEST in SHOW

This was a proud day for me showing and winning under a well-respected interstate Judge who was also a top breeder of beautiful collies.

CHAPTER 17

My shelties had settled well into kennel life and although I loved them all I did not have a favourite dog for some time, He was still to come. As the years passed by I had reluctantly come to a sad decision. I was feeling as if the collies were getting harder for me to do them justice with all the grooming as well as moving them to advantage in the show. It was with a very heavy heart that I found perfect homes for them all and even made my heart breaking decision to part with my Maggie. This was very difficult for me. However I bit the bullet and I rang my cousin Jessie who lived on her beautiful rural property in Denmark W.A. Jessie was grieving over losing her sheltie boy that I had given to her fifteen years before. He had been a special show dog but I was worried about his health as he had frightened me by taking several fits so was on tablets. This had never happened to any dog of mine in the past and so I decided that I would never use him at stud. I warned her when she decided that she wanted to have him that it would be a big risk as perhaps he would not have a long time to live. However with her loving care they had a happy life together plus to my knowledge he never had another fit during his long life. He was sixteen years old when he departed and Maggie was to be replacement for Jessie's lost companion. I knew that Jessie would love and care for her and they would be a perfect match. Waving goodbye with tears running down my cheeks I felt it was one of the saddest days of my life but I knew in my heart it was the best decision for Maggie, They both lived a very pleasant life for many years before Maggie died a peaceful death in her sleep. My darling Bonnie lived to be a very old lady before passing peacefully to the Rainbow Bridge where I hope to meet up with her and so many more of my favourite companions when my time comes.

This was Goodbye to my beloved Maggie

Chapter 18

The next episode was a quieter time for me as age was catching up too soon for my liking. I now was able to give my shelties all of my time and attention even though my age was beginning to give me a few problems. Running in the show ring was now more difficult and sadly not very pretty. This had been pointed out to me one day by a friend who advised me to get myself a handler to show my dogs. Apart from the ageing problem life for me was pretty good. I enjoyed my weekends at the show grounds with my dogs. I loved them all but one boy was very special to me. I had named him Thorpy after the Olympic swimming champion. He had a terrific temperament, loved people and enjoyed being in the show ring. I commissioned young Lass to be his handler; they made a very smart team in the ring. Each week he had two other males in his class of open dog, one being his litter brother. I had chosen to keep Thorpy because he had better colour marking and gave the other male to a friend to add to her team of show dogs. Every week these three open dogs competed keenly trying for top spot on the day. This made each show day quiteexciting as they seemed to all have their days to win. They battled it out overmany shows and eventually Thorpy became a champ Australian Champion Kismet the Thorpedo.

My friend Kaye who was the owner of his brother and a much keener exhibitor than me took her boy that she called "Roy" on to many more shows over a much longer period in fact this lovely dog was still showing, looking spectacular at nine years of age. This I believe could be a record for a sheltie male to still be winning at this age. I was a little bit proud that at least I was his breeder, however full credit goes to Kay, his owner for looking after him so well over the years not to mention the keenness to keep it up for so long.

My breeding plans were working out to my satisfaction. I now had a team of very lovely females that would be shown till they were approximately two years or they gained their championship status. They would then be retired from the ring to produce a litter out of which I would select one to keep that would hopefully improve and upgrade the line. The remaining pups would be sold to selected homes with a life time guarantee they were to be returned to me if any problems cropped up during their lifetime.

I was always on hand to give advice and help to the new owners if needed. Sometimes this took up many hours on the phone when inexperienced people had taken home the first puppy in their life. However I was happy to do this and never begrudged my time or attention. Dogs had given me so much joy that I wanted everyone to feel the same pleasure. After each girl had weaned her pups I would then search for the perfect forever home for her with a new family to love. The money I earned from selling the puppies at ten weeks of age covered some of the kennel expenses so I was enjoying the life I had chosen as well as making so many people happy to have a special dog in their lives. Looking after these puppies was enough to keep me occupied during the week days but weekends were not so satisfactory those days. I was frustrated watching handlers take my dogs running in the ring. As I sat watching the somewhat older people showing their dogs in the toy section the thought came that perhaps I could find a nice little dog from the toy group to show myself, as there was not much running involved in this ring. I noticed that there were a few oldies still showing their own toy dog. So what could I do about this I was sure there was an answer so I went searching again.

Chapter 19

I knew a little about small breeds as we had had a Pomeranian in Queensland who was Jeff's close companion after Ekka had passed on to the Rainbow bridge. Her name was Jenny, she followed him everywhere. It was so amusing to see the little red head pop up out of the long grass looking for him when they were in the paddock. As time went by she passed on and I was searching for another mate for Jeff. I decided after some research on small breeds to purchase a Bichon Frise. This was Samantha the bichon that had travelled with us when we came over from Queensland. I had come to the conclusion that if all Bichons were like this pretty but a very aloof dog I was not very fond of the breed. However she went about her assigned duties following obediently after Jeff not showing any emotion. After we had settled in W.A. we decided that perhaps having a litter might soften her nature and proceeded to find a suitable stud dog to do the deed. The plan was put into action Samantha produced the most gorgeous puppies, all snowy white with big black eyes. I was thrilled with them but unfortunately there was no change in her nature. She just plodded along in to old age being herself till she too passed over to the Rainbow Bridge years later. I had kept one of her pups naming her Julie. She became my special indoor companion with a sweet loving nature as opposite to her Dam as chalk is to cheese. Julie was with me happily for a long time until I discovered a lump on her neck. The vet diagnosed it as a fast growing tumour, a few weeks later he came again to put her to sleep in my arms. It was another sad tearful day as I placed her under a beautiful white camellia bush in the garden outside my bedroom window. I wonder if it still blooms now I am not living there.

THE RAINBOW BRIDGE • 71

Julie's last Day

Chapter 20

I found that there was a big demand for Bichon's at this time as they are valued as house hold pets in homes where there are allergy problems. The family's with allergy's can't have a normal dog or cat as a household pet but it has been proven that Bichon Frise are one of the exceptions. The main advantage is that these dogs have wool instead of hair so they do not shed to irritate allergy sufferers. A problem was starting to worry me at this time as with no income our money was getting low now I had no boarding dogs to pay for the upkeep of the kennels. This meant I had to find a means to cover costs of enjoying my own dogs. Breeding bichons seemed to me to be a good plan. I believed that these special little dogs would only make this world a better place for many family's that were missing out on the joy of owning a precious pet in their lives. I proceeded to buy several bichons to start me off on this new venture. Meeting new family's and having them visit several times while waiting for pups to reach the age that they could happily take them home was rewarding. All the time they waited I was able to educate the new owners to be, on all aspects of dog owner ship so they would be fully prepared to have a happy house hold when the time came for them to take on the responsibility of a new puppy? I often joked that my dear little babies were my bread and butter dogs as they helped pay for the dog food and the bills but I felt in my heart that I was doing a good thing by being able to spread a little joy into otherwise pet empty homes. I sometimes thought that although my Bichons would probably never be groomed up and show trained to win blue ribbons in the show ring they would be more valued in the homes I had selected for them. This made me feel as if I was doing a service not money grubbing.

Two of my bread and butter babies ready for their new homes

One morning I was expecting one of the bichons to soon deliver a big litter. I was taking her an early breakfast when as I stepped through the gate I noticed to my horror half a snake's body at my feet. I quickly counted heads of the dogs gathered around and at once knew what had happened. My pregnant girl had killed then eaten the other half of the snake. She would have reverted to nature and attacked the predator but died from poison she digested. This terrible happening made me realise that though these little dogs may seem to be all sweet and gentle they can also become savage if faced with danger to themselves or the pack. This snake was a deadly dugite and very poisonous.

Getting back to my task of finding a dog for me to show now I thought I was too old to show my own shelties, I got down to the serous search for the suitable breed to fit into my life style. I had bichons that were delightful but took too much time and effort to make ready for the show ring so mine were all pet Groomed (coats cut short).I took one to be shown once and decided it was too much effort to prepare to the standard of grooming needed to compete with the professionals

My only attempt to groom a Bichon at a show

It was very essential to me that there were no known inbred health problems in a breed I would consider owning. I know many breeds of pedigree dogs have these hidden faults that often show up later as the dog grows into maturity. This is very bad news for owners as well as dogs and sadly the vets are the only ones who profit. Finally I decided that the Papillion would be the chosen breed for me as these very beautiful intelligent little charmer's seemed to tick all the boxes I wanted. I set out to find one as my next project. Computers had by now become a useful tool in most homes including mine. I sat down to search for the next dog to help fill the gaps in my life. Once again I was very lucky and would you believe! Of all places in the country I found her in Queensland. This state was a magnet to me it seemed so back I went to meet my latest little dog. The breeder that I contacted was a very helpful lady named Nola who was a breeder of very lovely dogs. I am forever grateful to her for helping me get started with a lovely little female named Honey.

My New Baby Honey

I tried my luck in the Toy show ring with Honey but I must admit it was not the happy success that I had hoped as Honey did not enjoy the experiences at all. It had always been my opinion that if my dog was not happy in the ring with me it was kinder to let it stay home. Honey retired early and was mated in the hope that she would produce a keener participant for me to show. All this happened in the quiet time of the showing year and so by the next year Honey had produced a sweet little girl I named "Kismet Star Attraction" for me to proudly exhibit. I trotted her out in the ring and she performed very well. Honey at the age of almost fifteen years at this time as I write this now lives in this village with a friend that after losing her first little old dog now loves and cares for Honey. She still wanders around on her daily walk and is remarkable in her old age.

It did not take very long before I found that I was not enjoying the new company I was in with the toy people. It was not that anyone was unpleasant they were all quite nice to me but I sorely missed my old mates in the working dog ring and spending the days with collies and shelties. So I gave up my long time appearance on that stage with some regret. I am very thankful for the immense pleasure that I have gained over the many years I have enjoyed the company plus the excitement of competing for ribbons and trophies. It has been for the most part a very enjoyable and interesting time over many years and certainly not a boring way to spend my time.

Chapter 21

My husband Jeff had passed away after a long period of illness. He had a second heart operation and never really recovered to be the man he was before his heath had become a problem. I was now alone except for my many dogs sad feeling sad and unsure of what to do about it . When Jeff had become really ill I became his carer. This was a bad time for us both as he was not a very good patient and did not like following his doctor's orders. I must admit being a carer did not suit me very much either. There was a lot of work to be done around the property; There were also cat's coming in to board in the cattery and my dogs to care for. I knew it was all getting to much for me to cope with so decided to call for help from my cousin Joyce. She was very happy to come to my rescue as she was now a widow with time on her hands and feeling lonely.

I set her up to live in the cattery flat and help to look after the visiting cats. The plan that Jeff and I had dreamed up when we first settled back in WA was, as we aged we would move into the cattery flat to live ,boarding cats as an interest and income, leaving younger people to live in the big house and run the kennels. However life does not always follow up on the plans we make. I had presented Joyce with several very nice pedigree cats to introduce her to the show world of cats where I hoped she would meet new friends, something that I soon was to regret. Joyce had always been a besotted animal lover and a collector of unwanted pets. She took to her new life like a duck to water enjoying herself with the new mates she met at cat shows each weekend. She had moderate success with her cats and would come in beaming with excitement waving her ribbon if her cat had won a prize. She did have one big win with a cat that we had bought. It won best Exhibit at the Perth Royal, she had her photo with it in the paper, and that was a big thrill for her. It was so good to see her happy again.

A big problem was looming as Joyce kept gathering more cat owner friend's around her. She had always been a soft touch loving and trusting everyone. It wasn't long before the cat world knew that they had found a wonderful new dumping ground for their rejected cats. I discovered that every time I went over to see her I would spy another strange cat had arrived. Joyce would be so excited tme that a very kind friend had given it to her and surprisingly did not want for any money for it. The cattery that I had envisioned as being filled with paying guests was now a dead loss. Paying guests had disappeared as more hungry freeloaders took over. It was all too difficult for me as I loved my silly little cousin and truly hated to get tough and hurt her feelings. I did not know how to get her to see what she was doing much less how to stop her overcrowding the building with male cats that were creating a dreadful smell that was very difficult to endure. I was more than relieved when one of her friends offered her a home in exchange for looking after their cats. This solved the problem for me even though I was very upset that it had all gone pear shaped.

Joyce's health deteriorated several years later and my dear little cousin whom I had always been so close to passed away. We grew up as sisters from our early childhood. She is missed very much by me and all who loved her. I blame myself for a lot of what happened in the breakdown of our past relationship. I wish I had tried to be more direct and made sure that our future business was not compromised. Perhaps I could have got through to her that her behaviour in flouting the rules of never housing male undoctored cats was not on. I now regret that I was not strict about this. I had known that if she felt she was being criticised she would be very hurt and I could not do that to her. So we both paid the price for my hesitation. However it is useless to regret the past mistakes if you can't change them

Joyce with the Qld cat we bought for her to show

Chapter 22

Around this time a friend named Tanya with her family had moved in to my house and kennels while I had tried living in her house in the suburbs on an arrangement that my dogs that I still had would be looked after. I would take two of them at a time with me on a rotating system for company. I would have my mother's while they had their pups so I would be with them to give them any help they sometimes need while whelping. This was a good scheme in theory however it did not work out so well in practise.

I felt lonely in the suburbs, there were no friendly neighbours to chat to as it seemed everyone went off to work. It all came to a sticky end when the only neighbour that did not go to work popped his head over the high fence and saw that that day I had more than the allotted number of two dogs in the yard. He wasted no time reporting me to the Council Ranger who also popped his head over the fence to check on my yard. He had climbed on a box to spy on my back yard then knocked on the front door to tell me that it was against the law to keep more than two dogs. All that was too much for me I had to get back to the kennel zone so a new plan was dreamed up. I decided to build a granny flat on the disused corner portion of the kennel property facing the same way as the cattery with a fenced area for my own dogs. I did this then arranged for Tanya to buy the property at a reduced price with a contract that I could live there rent free for ten years. I reasoned that at eighty years of age I might be ready to give up my interests. This time passed quickly and it was with mixed feelings I started to part with all my beloved dogs and all the belongings that had been necessary to maintain this lifestyle I had been enjoying over so many busy years. It was time to move on.

About this time I met a man who was keen to escort me to bingo fund raising events for the club. We had a few other outings and he soon decided that I should be his full time companion in the future. It took him some time to persuade me that this would be a good idea. I started to think that perhaps as he was five years younger than me it might be good to have someone in my life to take care of me in my old age   This turned out to be another bad joke that fate had in store for me.

A few years later when some of my family were coming to visit from Queensland we made the decision to get married. Instead of the registry office quiet ceremony that I thought would be appropriate for a eighty year old couple it was decided by our lovely Village manager" Janice" (who just happened to be a marriage celebrant) that we should do it in style in the Jacaranda garden setting. This idea caught on like fire and was a tremendous success. Someone remarked it was a nice change for the residents to the wakes that were a little more common around the village. It was a really wonderful day in September with the weather being favourable and the gardens and decorations spectacular. All the village residents and many of my friends came to join in the celebrations enjoying the day. The ladies of the village provided lots of delicious food for the wedding breakfast. It really was a day in my life that I enjoyed to the brim. Having so many friends and family joining me in such a happy time was a blessing that will always be a cherished memory. My eldest son Kerry flew over from Queensland to give me away. He joked that he had done that many years ago.   All of Bob's very nice family attended to wish us luck and we all enjoyed this special day. We settled down to many happy times in the future together. Once again fate foiled my plan as my loving man developed "Parkinson's" and his health soon was a big problem. We had a few reasonable years and had some good times travelling with our very pleasant friendly neighbours. We visited in Queensland to introduce Bob to the rest of my family, he impressed everyone that we stayed with his talent of being a top handy man to have visiting

All too soon it came to an end and I found myself again in the hated role of being a carer to an invalid. My love, Bob passed away in March 2020 after being cared for in the last months of his life in a nursing home where he was happy to be enjoying the attention from very special people. It had become impossible for me to lift him from his constant falls. My health was starting to fail under the strain of watching him in such distress. In one way it was a relief to see him slip away. In my heart I said a silent thank you to whoever decides that the time had come for his pain and frustration to come to an end, "Parkinson's" is such a cruel fate for someone to fall victim to. I had a tall strong athletic man to love me for a few short years before he was stolen away with a dreadful disease to become a helpless invalid that I would have to push in a wheelchair. I am grateful that I am gifted now with very good health and do not suffer many problems that so many people of my age do. Perhaps I have been lucky but I do feel that as my life has been so busy with so many loved dogs to care for I just have not had time to get old and decrepit yet. I hope and pray that that I still have several more years to experience some other exciting adventures.

My wedding day September 2008

This was taken the very last time Bob was able to be brought home to me. It gave us the chance to watch our favourite football team "The Eagles "win the Premiership for WA together

Chapter 23

So now I am all alone again except for my little dog in our beautiful Lifestyle village Jacaranda Gardens, living with my memories and my remaining little Papillion "Star" who sits faithfully at my side and moves with me into each part of this small villa where we live in what now seems a retirement village. She has become my boss who guards me with all her tiger like energy against all comers on our daily walks. She is wonderful company and I cannot imagine what I would do if I lost her. I am happy that as we age we are still quite sprightly and are often told that people cannot believe we are both very old ladies. I keep busy with my painting, enjoying the company of the many wonderful friends I have now that I have become a member of an Art Society I have even progressed to selling a few paintings mostly of other people's dogs but I try many different ways of expressing my talents for my own amusement. I am enjoying the company of so many lovely people who help me be happy in my final adventures in the latter stage of this exciting life and in my last remaining years

Life is still good. Writing down these precious memories of the many years filled with dogs that I have loved has been another pleasure for me, I have very much enjoyed the time spent remembering the past so much in fact I have dipped deep in my memory box and put to paper another adventures that I experienced because of my time with my dogs. I do hope you enjoy reading my long story as much as I have remembering it all.

CHAPTER 24

Past Memories

In 1998 I had a very special adventure to add to my memories of my life living with my many dogs and the friends that I gathered because of them. At this time I was living in Canning vale W.A. at my kennel property, breeding my show dogs and exhibiting them in shows each weekend. I also travelled interstate several times each year to show my shelties, I would meet up with friends and enjoy many successes and sometimes disappointments along the way.

I had been breeding Bichon Fris`e to sell to family's who because of allergy or other problems could not have an ordinary puppy. This part of my life brought me a lot of satisfaction as I met with so many very special families who were happy to take my advice re choosing a big asset into their lives by the purchase of a little white bundle of love. Usually I would get a phone call inquiring about a puppy, telling me that their child was allergic to many things but hoping that a puppy would be the exception. On several occasions I met people who had children who were terrified of dogs. After a few visits to get to know firstly the babies then adults and with me explaining how to deal with their fear it was so good to see each child's confidence develop. I would invite family's to visit me to see the puppies before they were ready to go to new homes in order to decide if they were ready to take on a pet. This strategy proved to be a big success as well as a relief for me to know that I matched up families with the pet that would bring so much pleasure into their lives. It also was enjoyable for me to get to know more people apart from my dog show friends who sometimes were a mixed blessing because of our competing in the show ring each weekend. Sometimes a bit of jealousy would pop up to spoil the days outing.

    I had met a lovely young lady named Kathy who came from Singapore and visited when she came to Perth. She was on a trip with other people that were members of the Singapore kennel Club. They were interested in finding some extra information from other dog owners. Because I was a breeder of Shetland Sheepdogs and also Collie (R) I was the one that Kathy found to ask about solutions to help her deal with her collie's ear problem. I was able to show her a few tricks to help, we became instant friends. Sometime later in the year I was visited by another Singapore lady on holiday, who was interested in buying a Bichon puppy to take home with her. I sadly told her that I could not help her at present as I did not have any pups for sale but if she wished I would let her know when one was available and make sure it could be freighted to her when it was ready. About this time I had a phone call from Kathy asking me to find her a young Sheltie for her grandmother who wanted one to keep her company. Kathy also hopefully asked if I could pick one that she could show at the local shows. I told her I had the perfect one to suit both her and

    Her Grandma. His name was Nova and he was a young male just out of minor puppy class he had been to several shows performed well however the big white blaze on his face was unfortunate as this marking was not fashionable at this time in the Sheltie world here. However, the judge for the last big show was a very highly regarded judge from Singapore. He loved white blazes and also loved the puppy that he was judging on the day. He awarded him Puppy in Show as his prize. The girl that was handling him was over the moon but she was devastated when I told her that I was sending him to Kathy, this would be his last show in Australia. He was leaving on the only burst of glory he would ever have here but would likely have a better chance in his new country. This event would lead to an exciting new adventure for me.

Chapter 25

I had entertained a Baroness from Germany who had judged our first Collie National Show (A very big deal in the Dog World) This prestigious event was run by the WA Collie Club of which I was on the committee at this time. After the show was over I came home to discover one of my pregnant Sheltie girls was in labour. She was a very special blue merle and I was worried that she was in trouble as she stopped pushing after the first three babies. I knew that there were more to come so at 2am I was at the vet while two more blue babies were delivered. All was well with Mother and bubs but I couldn't say the same for me. I was exhausted but I had promised to pick up our lady judge The Baroness and entertain her. This did not prove difficult as every time she was missing, I would find her with the new mother and babies. The Baroness who asked me to call her Dina was thrilled as she had never seen a blue litter before. She was very impressed by this one and enjoyed spending time with them while she was with me. However, I was not very happy as this was the second time this girl had given me the trouble and expense of having to take her for help delivering in the early hours. So I said never again, I would find her a pet home after getting her spayed. Later that day Dina said she would love to take Blue girl home with her, or rather I could send her after she had weaned the pups. I told her that would be a silly idea as the expense would be very high. This girl had had two problem mating's and her show career was over. So what was the point? I could see that she was disappointed with my reasoning. I suggested that if she would like to have a blue girl that she could show I would breed another litter from this girl sending her the pick of the litter if there was a suitable girl produced. I secretly thought she would forget all about it by the time she got home but I was mistaken. I soon started to get letters from Germany reminding me of my promise; she was keeping me to it. Time went by and when the next season came for Blue Girl to be mated I remembered my promise. I picked the top tricolour male available, mated her much against my better judgement. However to my joyful surprise Blue girl delivered a beautiful litter of six puppies with no effort, all on her own, even a perfectly marked blue merle girl for the Baroness. Fate this time was smiling on me.

Kismet Symphony in Blue

Chapter 26

I had a very special friend in Finland named Sari whom I had met when she was a young lass who came to Australia to spend time with her Aussie boyfriend quite a few years before. She was a breeder of shelties in Finland and missed them very much while she was here. I would often find her in the kennels sitting cuddling one of my girls, especially one I called Blossom. One day I received a phone call from Sari. She told me that there would be a huge World Show in Helsinki in 1998 and I should come and visit. My mind started to buzz with an idea. My lady from Singapore now wanted to buy two bichons, I had also the Sheltie for Kathy as well as the blue puppy for Dina. They would all be due to fly around the same time as "The World show in Finland". The stage was set for my big adventure.as I had decided to take them all with me as passenger's luggage and deliver them myself to the new owners

It was all arranged with tickets bought and big plans made for the trip of my life the first stop would be Singapore. Today started at 4.30 am with a wakeup call. I dress and go to the kennel to let out Nova and Symphony (The Shelties) to have a three quarter hour run before the big trip. I carry up the two bichon puppies; have a quick cuppa before the transport arrives to take us to the airport en route to Helsinki to show at the world show.I had never imagined I could be part of such an exciting event; it was so hard to believe that we were really going .I see the dogs into the cargo department then we were on our way. The flight was interesting as I was seated with two judges that I knew quite well. They were also going to see the World Show as spectators so were interested to know that I would be competing with my Sheltie puppy. This was the puppy that I had saved for the Baroness. I named her Symphony and she was a very nice blue well up to standard for the show ring. I had sent many photos of Symphony to Dina in Germany to make sure that she still wanted to have this puppy. The deal that I made with her was that she pays for my flight from Helsinki to Germany as payment for Symphony. She was very happy with this deal so this agreement was satisfactory to us both.

In Singapore it was very hot outside of the beautiful terminal when we arrived. We were treated to a very enthusiastic welcome from the new puppy owner's lead by Kathy. She had contacted the Bichon buyers and they were all very excited waiting to see their new babies. Kathy is a special person and though I had only met her once before she took charge marched us like an army through all the proceedings. Firstly we had to go to another place to where Symphony had been sent as she was to go on with the next part of the journey. Before we could proceed we had to queue in line to receive passes to go through into the huge complex where cargo from all over the world was being moved around. It was organised chaos. After many wrong directions we finally found Symphony. She was pleased to see me but scared of all the noise. We were able to take her to a small space of grass so she could relive herself. Poor little baby it must have been so frightening to be amongst the noise of fork lifts all buzzing around her. Reluctantly I had to push her back in the crate gave her fresh water then we went on to find the bichon babies also Nova the ten month old Sheltie that was to be Kathy's grandmothers companion. There was more running around to please all the official little men from the customs. Finally the crates were brought in to us. The babies were so pleased to see all the admiring people that had come to rescue them from the long confinement. They gave all the new owners and friend's big tongue kisses. Kathy was thrilled to see Nova, she was so happy that he had got there completely none fazed by the long trip and ready to be friends. Thank God I have bred good temperaments in my dogs. After giving the bichon people lots of advice on caring for their new pets I said good bye to all. We got into Kathy's beautiful car speeding off away from the airport to her home for a nice shower and a cup of tea. Forty minutes later there we were being greeted by her tri colour collie (the love of Kathy's life.)The collie met the new arrival with a mixture of come hither but touch me not which was so cute to see, I knew they would soon be good mates. Nova displayed all his many charms to the new family. They were amazed by his perfect ears lovely thick shiny coat and especially his thick white collar with his big white blaze. Kathy immediately decided he would be a Singapore champion. Poor Grandma had lost her dog before she had even seen him. The rest of the day was spent sightseeing, spending time with Kathy's family. Soon it was time for Symphony with a very tired me to depart to continue on our way to Finland to the next part of this big adventure. I was so happy to arrive in Finland to be greeted by my very special friend Sari and her lovely family again. This was my second visit to them; the last one was quite a few years before. That time spent with Sari had given me some wonderful memories that I will treasure for the rest of my life.

On my first visit to Finland with my cousin Joyce we had spent three weeks with them as part of our round the world trip. We had a really wonderful time in spite of lack of sleep due to the strangeness of day and night being as one. I think the people would be talking all night, never getting to bed at all in the summer time. I expect this was in compensation for the coming short dark days of winter that were coming. Sari was waiting to see if she had passed her examination to be able to enter university Veterinary school. She told me that she very nervous as very few applicants were accepted each year. There was always a frightening wait to see if you would be one of the successful people. Previously she had asked me to find her a border collie in Australia to send to her as she wanted to show and work trials with one. I had found a dog that I hoped would be suitable so I arranged for him to be sent to her. This was twelve months before and she was very happy with my choice. His name was Ace and he settled in to his new life very well. He was a beloved companion house dog by the time we arrived for our time with the family. Ace was being handled by a young man in the show ring; much to Sari's delight was doing very well. Sari was in a lot of pain with her leg as she had damaged it in a bad fall. She had difficulty running so was not able to show him herself hence needing a handler. There was a big show coming up in a town next to the Swedish border that Ace as well as Sari's little sheltie boy were entered. So off we went for me to see what the difference between shows here and at home were. Sari told me that her usual handler would not be available to show Ace and asked me if I would mind taking him in to be judged. This made me very happy to get the chance to show Ace as border collies were my first breed that started me off in the Dog World many years before. So I raced down to the shop, bought myself a pair of running shoes. Putting on a tee shirt that I had brought with me with a map of Australia in flies as a pattern on the front and a pair of jeans to complete the outfit. Back home I would never go to a show looking like that as dress up was required to compliment your dog in the ring. However I thought no one would notice me as it was only a border collie I was to show, a breed that was hardly ever was considered for top placing's in the show ring.

    We set off next morning at 3am with the sun on high to drive the 3 hour journey to the town where the show was to be held. I would never have dreamed that this was the start of the most wonderful dog show days of my life. I was to have this terrific day at my first Dog Show in Finland. We arrived at the show grounds and found a familiar scene of dogs being vetted by busy vets making sure all the entrees were fit and no bitches in season sneaking through to excite the other males. The only difference was the chatter in language that I could not understand a word but they could certainly chatter? Soon it was time for the serious part of the judging of the border collies. I was pleased to see that the judge for this section was a top Australian Championship Judge that I had watched many times but did not know personally. I took Ace into the ring with several others in the same class. I moved around the ring with Ace then standing him for the judge to examine. I was directed to the first place in the class. Sari was very excited so happy with my handling and the win. At dog shows in Europe after a judge decides on the winning exhibit (or perhaps it is every exhibit) he or she has to dictate a critique to the ring steward the reason that dog has been chosen for this placing. Ace's critique also stated that he was well handled so this earned a pat on the back for me from Sari.

The next thrill for her was the Sheltie class; much to her joy the little Sheltie won his class, and then went on, gaining the points to make him a champion and Best of breed on the day. Then it was back to the Border collie ring. Ace and I had to do our turn again, moving round at a smart pace, Ace felt so good on the lead. The judge apparently thought so as well as we were given a sash together with a handshake so I decided we must have won. I could not understand a word but Sari was jumping up and down in excitement. By this time I was getting rather tired but there was more to come. We had to wait for a few hours till all dogs had been judged, then all Best of breed winners were assembled. It was a long day, I was a little confused by all that was going on in frantic chatter but it became clear that Ace was to be lined up again. I stood in line with all the winning dogs of each section. I was amazed at the long line ups. Some breeds were completely unknown to me. Each dog was looked at in turn, run or walked round the full ring twice before being placed in one of the three places to the side. I stood legs aching wondering what happens next as it all was so different to our shows at home.

Finally after what seemed ages Ace had his turn. As we came to a stop the judge pointed to us. A roar went up from the onlookers and the loud speakers called out in an excited gabble the only words I could understand was "Border Collie Australia" Could it be I had been on the lead of a BEST In SHOW winner? In an all breeds huge show. Yes it was true. It was to be the one and only time in my long career as a dog handler or owner exhibitor. How amazing it was to be in such a hallowed place dressed in my tee shirt decorated with Aussie flies. How I wish I had a photo in my get up with the huge bouquet I was clutching after being presented with it. My friend Sari was beside herself with joy she came running into the ring to hug me then Ace. She then flung her arms round the judge when he came over to talk. It all seems a bit over the top now so many years have gone by and hard to believe how carried away by the thrill we had that day by the big win. I am so grateful that I have these special memories. This wonderful day we had was only topped by the terrific news when we arrived back at her home. It was that Sari had a letter saying she had won a place to study Veterinary Science in the university and that she would be enrolled for the next course. It all seemed like an unbelievable dream.

Chapter 27

Back to 1998 and visiting Finland, it was wonderful to see my friends again when I arrived with Symphony. It felt like it was no time since we had been together to talk about dogs nonstop. Sari was by now an almost qualified Veterinary Practitioner with only her final examination to complete before going out on her own to start earning money.

We had a week before the World Show so Sari, Symphony and I decided to go to her home in Toyvaka to stay with her family before coming back to Helsinki for the big day. Sari said I would need a certificate to prove Symphony was clear of hip dysplasia. This was necessary for German Kennel club as the Baroness would need this if she wanted to breed with her in the future. The German kennel Club were very strict about this but it was not so in Australia in those days. Luckily for me Sari had invested with a friend in a practise so I did not have to pay a fee for the scans. It was done and the results were very good, her score was high so that was a blessing.

My dear little friend Sari would never get the full benefits from all her hard earned work studying to become fully qualified as her health became a big problem. Her leg that she had damaged as a young girl never stopped giving her terrible pain for many years. After countless stays in hospital and very constant severe pain it was at last amputated. The news that she had passed on to her Rainbow Bridge came to me via Facebook.

It breaks my heart to remember how much she suffered in her short life but was she was always surrounded by her beloved dogs her loving family and many friends who loved her. She did not deserve what she had to bear. It makes me very sad to think I never had the chance to say goodbye to her.

This is the last picture I took of Sari before I left Finland on my way to Germany

CHAPTER 28

The World Show Helsinki 1998

This was held in a huge complex all marble and shining green carpet with people and dogs everywhere. Polite reserved but friendly helpful people with dogs to match it seemed. There was every kind of dog I had ever heard of yet so many that I had to ask "What breed is that" They were all so well behaved and obedient. Once inside I was dismayed to find that the sheltie ring was so far away from the Border collie area. I was left in the care of one of Sari's friend who luckily spoke English very well. She was able tell me what the procedure would be. The Finnish show ring felt very strange so different to what I was used to at home. There was no Gate Stewards to call out your number to line you up. There was a Ring Steward who ticked your number off but where to stand? I asked and was vaguely waved into position. So the Sheltie judging was commencing.

The World Show 1998

The judge was Paivie Errolli a Sheltie breeder that Sari had introduced me to last time I was in Finland years before. Symphony was first to be judged also the first time she had ever been to a show. I did not know how she would behave in such a different atmosphere or any other experience. However much to my amazement she took one look around and it was as though she had decided "I know what to do" she never put a foot wrong. Giving a polite greeting to Paivi she moved around the ring like a dream. I was so proud and happy that after all I had put this young pup through to get her here to have her perform so well. She well deserved the first place, beating all the others in her class. This meant we would have to move on to the Best in Group ring at the end of the day. At this gigantic show there were 15600 dogs entered, 300 different breeds from 44 countries. It is the Olympics of the Dog Word. Just imagine here we were in the heart of all the excitement of it and one humble West Aussie Dog breeder with a blue merle home bred Shetland sheepdog. I felt as I was living in a dream. The time soon came for us to compete with all the other best entries of each breed.

We were all assembled on an enormous stage surrounded by tiers of seats filled with spectators. There were spotlights moving over the stage and it looked for all the world like a movie set. We all sat in the wings waiting for our cue to perform. I made friends with a little blue merle Cardigan corgi from England who was to go in after Symphony. There were some outstanding puppies from groups known and unknown to me. The puppy in front of us was a little black long coated happy larrikin of a breed I did not recognise. He came from Denmark. There was a really lovely German shepherd also that I thought would have a good chance to win. However to my surprise and delight Symphony was picked as first place and I was given I was given the trophy. I was so unsure of how this system worked as I was in a daze I just went were they pointed me to go. All the pups were prejudged before going into the big ring on the stage by a very pleasant happy judge who joked with me about my accent and kept calling me Aussie. We were not given any results.

The large crowd heartily applauded every dog as we paraded. Once again Symphony to my delight performed well she showed herself off to perfection. There were 44 in the class; Symphony was in the first 10 finalists for best in show. I was happy with that result we certainly were not disgraced. I came home with a very pretty glass vase, Symphony's trophy for winning Best Puppy in World Show Helsinki. It is my treasured memento of that very Special Day.

Now we were to have two weeks of fun in Finland. Sari also had success with her border collies and the champagne was flowing as we all celebrated a terrific time at this fabulous World show. Now it was over but I was left with so many wonderful memories of many new and old friends that I had time with as well as the magnificent dogs I had seen. It was truly an education also one of the most thrilling events of my long life. So now I had two weeks to spend with Sari to enjoy the scenery and generous hospitality of the very special Finnish people that I was so fond of. I discovered the difference between our two countries in how our dogs were treated in general. Here in Finland they were truly one of the family and a big part of their lives. They travel on public transport almost everywhere that the family go in their daily lives. There are no sad lonely dog refuges as we have in our part of the world. If a dog proves unsuitable to the new owners (A very rare thing) a network of friends, breeders etc. take over and a more suitable home is found, there is no dumping of pets in Finland. I was to spend family time with Sari and Parents Turtu & Seppo. On June the 20th it is the first day of the mid-summer festival holiday. It is celebrated with the raising of the flag to the mast outside of each home and the placing of birch branches along the front path. I never did work out the significant reason for this. In the evening a huge bonfire is lit. There are sausages being cooked on long sticks with many friends and neighbours joining in the fun.

Sari's Mother and Father Raising the Flag

After the fires burn down families retire to their saunas where it is tradition to take branches of birch leaves with which everyone whips each other all over. I was a little alarmed at this prospect but to my surprise I found the birch leaves were quite soft and pleasant on the body, the scent was delightful. It was all a very interesting experience.

Most family's travel for a few days break after this to their summer cottages in the Forrest always on the edge of a lake. I visited several of Sari's friends at their summer cottages and was made to feel very welcome. I was offered all the traditional treats offered by the people who were very pleased if you enjoyed them. One lovely day there was a very enjoyable trip on a ferry around the largest lake in Finland. The car went on the ferry's we climbed up a flight of stairs finding ourselves in a cafe with beautiful hanging baskets filled with flowers. There was lots of pine tables and benches all glassed in so we could see the passing scenery. We watched little islands with summer cottages partly hidden by tall pine trees complete with separate saunas and landings for people to plunge in the cold lake after steaming in the saunas I think this is why everyone I met had rosy perfect complexions. In the houses I visited, the ladies all sauna together naked, then it is the men of the family's turn. However at one home when I was asked "Would I sauna" I think I saw an impish light in one dear old gentleman's eyes when he asked me the standard question. Luckily for me my hostess who had arranged the visit declined politely saying that we had other visits to make that day so we had to leave. Australian's seemed to be a novelty to our hosts. So many of the younger people speak beautiful English but the older generation did not. I found it very hard to communicate with them but a lot of fun.

One day I was kitted up in wellington boots with rain gear for a three and a half kilometre tramp in the forest. Oh! Boy! Was it forest? Through puddles over slippery rocks, through waist high wet grass that hit me in the face "Very invigorating" I said. Under my breath I thought something different. The three border collies plus the little sheltie loved it. I had my reservations but kept them to myself.

Sari had a very sad phone message that night to tell that one of her friends Irish Setters had been involved in an accident. It had run into a passing motor bike and been killed. Sari was called out to see the dead dog and provide a Vets death certificate as this is necessary there, when a show dog dies. A big day was planned for a visit to people who owned thirteen Italian Grey hounds for Sari to scale their teeth for a big show the next weekend. Then we were to visit a winery for a wine tasting. I was told that as grapes did not grow in such a cold climate berries were used instead. It tasted very nice and I had several glasses. In the evening we were visited by five Hungarian Vizier dogs. Then we went on to a trial with borders and sheltie's together with other breeds to track in the forest. This is another official test available to dogs. They are sent out with messages returning between two handlers a kilometre apart three times. There were three dogs competing but Sari's Border collie was the only one to pass the test. We had another Celebration.

All too soon my unforgettable very doggy time in Finland was over and my preparations for flying to Germany were confirmed. I said a sad farewell to my beloved friend Sari, family and friends trying not to think too much about the chance that we would never be together again. Sadly we never were. Sari passed away recently after many years of suffering with her injured leg. A few years ago it was amputated so I hope she spent some time free from pain. I am always thankful for years that she was my treasured friend together with the lovely memories of times spent together.

Last day in Finland

Chapter 29

Germany was the next stop. I was on my way to the next adventure with Symphony sitting on my knee in the plane. This was very different to the way she had travelled from Australia in a crate in the cargo hold. While chatting to the hostess as we took off I mentioned that my fellow dog friends at home would be amazed how different it was to fly in Europe for little dogs. She was quiet shocked at the thought of putting them in with the cargo saying it was too cruel to think about.

We arrived in Frankfurt airport. I did not have any idea of what to do to find Dina (The Baroness) or even how to get out of the airport. I struggled out of the plane carrying Symphony trying to look like she was very light as eight kilos was the limit on cabin luggage. When we got out of the plane I took her out of the dog bag, put on her lead then proceeded to try and find our way out of this gigantic almost empty place. I could not see any official looking person to ask. So we walked miles it seemed with the dog trotting beside me. Finally I stopped a well-dressed business type man and asked him if he spoke English. "Yes I do" he replied. "How do I get my luggage from the plane from Finland "I asked? He replied "I don't know". So that was that. I kept looking and walking then finally found a stairway to go down steps to find my lonely suit case going round and round all on its own. Onward we went through customs showing my passport as well as Symphony's rabies vaccination papers. I had to answer lots of questions. Finally I was waved through the barriers, at last I was free to find a very worried Dina who wondered what had happened to me as she thought I had disappeared forever. We made our way to the car park to find a magnificent Mercedes that was to be driven by a very nice young man who Dina had recruited to bring her to find me and drive us part of the way back to her place The country side was beautiful or what I could see of it as we sped along the Autobahn (Freeway) at terrific speed. It was many kilometres to Crotorff where Dina lived before I sorted myself out to realise what was going to happen. One hour later we arrived at a work place of the young man who had driven the car. He told me he had two collie dogs that the Baroness had bred for him and he was very happy with them. So I guess that the ride in the fabulous Mercedes was a return favour. I said Goodbye thanking him for the ride then let Symphony have a quick walk on the grass before getting into Dina's small car for the last lap of this journey. As we drove into a tree filled park like area I was to think my eyes were deceiving me. Before me was a huge castle surrounded by a moat looking like a picture in a child's story book.

Dina and some of her many dogs

Taking a stroll around the castle

Dina's Home

Dina drove on a little way till we came to a smaller version of the castle with a path leading to a stone stair way and huge old doors which was the entrance to Dina's home. She turned a giant key in the door which opened with a loud creaking sounding as in 'The Adams family' T V show I used to watch . Talk about creepy; it was hard to take in all that I was looking at. The floors were bare and there was a big stairway looming upwards to a landing with what looked like big fluffy grey mats on it. As I stared the mats suddenly came to life and turned into two of the tallest dogs I had ever seen. I think they were Borzoi or Irish wolf hounds but all I remember of them was size and the silence of them. They were so quiet and regal looking. As I looked around I could see knight's suits of armour standing, long cobwebs dangling everywhere. It was like a stage set for a horror movie. However, my hostess Dina and I seemed to be the only inhabitants apart from the dogs. On the subject of dogs, before going into the living part of this home, Dina had taken Symphony and I around the back of the building leading to an underground cellar. On opening the door there came what seemed to be a flood of dozens of collies and Shelties streaming out running around enjoying their freedom after their confinement. I was amazed and told Dina that I could not understand why she needed another dog when she already had so many. The rest of that evening was a bit of a blur, we had a meal in the kitchen that was a bare room with a standing wood stove, a cupboard and two chairs beside an uncovered table. I thought to myself that the outside of this wonderful building certainly gave no clues on what was inside. However I could find no fault in my hostess who was very sweet and welcoming.

My room was warm and the bed very comfortable so comfy that I slept like a log only to be wakened by the most terrifying scream from outside my window. I jumped out of bed looking out to see a peacock staring at me from the branch of the tree outside. That day Dina took me on the tour to visit fellow collie and sheltie breeders in the district. This was a nice round of ladies that mostly spoke English much better than my Australian. We did lots of looking and complimenting as well as drinking tea and eating all sorts of local treats that the ladies insisted that I try. This was fun. I also enjoyed admiring the shelties and collies owned by them.

Visiting in Germany

Chapter 30

I was enjoying my time on this very exciting adventure but it all came to an end the second night of my stay. I was awakened by Dina in the very early hours with a phone in her hand to say one of my sons was ringing me with bad news. My youngest son Leon had been in an accident and had been put in an induced coma. The news was he would be brought out of it in a week's time only then would the Doctors would know if he would live or not. I seemed to be in limbo on the flight home. There was a bit of confusion before the flight that I could not understand at the gate to the boarding line but I went through after a conference about my ticket and was soon settled for the long trek home.

Arriving back home I soon discovered that the mix up with my ticket was the reason for the entire problem in Germany; I had a ticket for the previous day. How that happened was a mystery, I was lucky to be allowed on the plane. I arrived back in the early morning. I came through Customs to find my little cousin Joyce waiting for me in a very distraught state as she had been expecting me to arrive the day before according to my schedule. She informed me that I was to judge at a show that day. I had completely forgotten all about, I would have to fulfil my contract as it would go badly against me if I did not cover my obligations, no excuse would let me off. So I rushed home showered and dressed and did my duty in a complete daze. I do not have any memory of that show but must have done a reasonable job as I was not bombarded by angry dog owners after it finished. No one had questioned me on why I had put their dog down when it was better than the awful dog I had favoured. This sometimes happened at the end of the judging. Sometimes it can be a problem finding the diplomatic answers to calm the egos of the upset owners.

Joyce had been busy on the phone talking to the airlines about my sad story of my son's accident in Queensland. She talked them into a free trip that evening going direct to Qld then on to Toowoomba I was upgraded to business class so; she must have given them a really good story about me being there when they awakened him. As it happened when I arrived at the hospital I found him sitting in a chair connected to lots of wires looking sad and sorry but alive. I talked to the Doctor about his condition and I was told that he was lucky that the truck that had squashed him flat against a wall had missed any vital parts of his body by inches. It was very fortunate that he was quite over weight around his girth; this had protected him, saving his life. The doctor advised me there would be no after affects to his body from this accident.

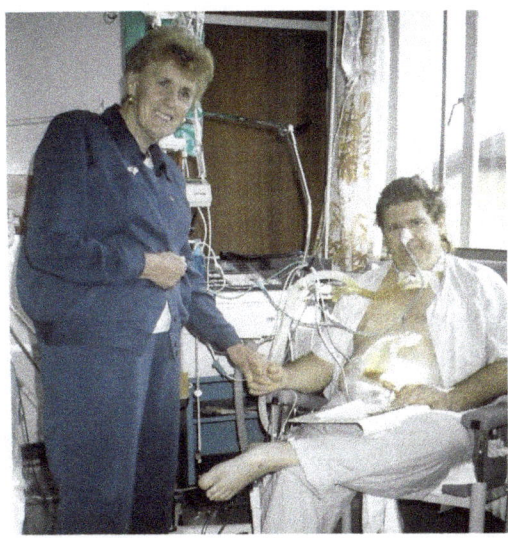

My reunion with Leon in Toowoomba Hospital

This part of my adventure I could have done without. I said a prayer of thankfulness that it ended so well and that I had arrived homes safely to start investigating what else the future had in store for me and the dogs in my life. Here are my thoughts now this book is finished.

I sometimes have the feeling that perhaps a guardian angel was looking after me while I was enjoying the interesting adventures I have had. I am deeply grateful for all wonderful people I have met along the way. Especially those who have kept me safe while I travelled far from my home as well as the lovely new friends who were so kind to me and made me feel so welcome in their lives and homes. They all will live in my heart in memory forever.

Post Script If some of my fellow dog people reading this book notice anything I have put into this missive that might be slightly different to facts they remember please forgive me and put any mistakes down my ninety two year old brain slipping a little trying to recall so many things I wanted to write about

Sincerely Pat Atkins

ABOUT THE AUTHOR

Pat Atkins at ninety two years of age now resides in Canningvale, Western Australia with her little dog "Star". She has many memories of her early life in Queensland and her introduction to the Dog world of Border collies exhibiting and sheepdog trials. Also of memories of beloved Collie (R) and Shelties, her travels and friends that she made over many years. She writes of her happy and sad times over a long but enjoyable and active life.

www.ingramcontent.com/pod-product-compliance
Lightning Source LLC
Chambersburg PA
CBHW061604110426
42742CB00039B/2835